MW01074482

★ A NAVY ADMIRAL'S BRONZE RULES ★

14 September 2021

VADM Sean Buck,

From a Ben Davis H.S. graduate to one from North Central -- case studies about the importance of integrity and leadership. If your staff is interested, I have mimeographed presentations to reinforce several of the case studies.

Dave Oliver

A NAVY ADMIRAL'S

BRONZE
RULES

MANAGING RISK
AND LEADERSHIP

REAR ADM. DAVE OLIVER, USN (RET.)

Naval Institute Press
Annapolis, Maryland

Naval Institute Press
291 Wood Road
Annapolis, MD 21402

© 2021 by Dave Oliver
All rights reserved. No part of this book may be reproduced or utilized
in any form or by any means, electronic or mechanical, including
photocopying and recording, or by any information storage and retrieval
system, without permission in writing from the publisher.

Library of Congress Cataloging-in-Publication Data

Names: Oliver, Dave, 1941– author.
Title: A navy admiral's bronze rules : managing risk and leadership / by Rear
  Admiral David Rogers Oliver, USN (Ret.)
Description: Annapolis, [MD] : Naval Institute Press, [2021]
Identifiers: LCCN 2019051455 | ISBN 9781682477212 (hardback) | ISBN
  9781682477366 (ebook) | ISBN 9781682477366 (epub)
Subjects: LCSH: Leadership—United States. | United States. Navy
  Submarine Forces—Anecdotes. | Organizational behavior—United States.
  | Corruption—United States—Prevention. | Organizational effectiveness—
  United States. | Admirals—United States—Biography. | United States.
  Navy Submarine Forces—Biography. | United States—History, Military—
  Anecdotes.
Classification: LCC VB203 .O76 2020 | DDC 303.3/4—dc23
LC record available at https://lccn.loc.gov/2019051455

♾ Print editions meet the requirements of ANSI/NISO z39.48–1992
(Permanence of Paper).
Printed in the United States of America.

29 28 27 26 25 24 23 22 21   9 8 7 6 5 4 3 2 1
First printing

The views expressed in this publication are those of the author and do
not necessarily reflect the official policy and position of the Department of
Defense or the U.S. government. The public release clearance of this publication by the Department of Defense does not imply Department of Defense
endorsement or factual accuracy of the material.

I met Linda Bithell one afternoon in the Bitton-Tuohy's Men's Store in Blackfoot, Idaho. I asked her to marry me on our first date. She turned me down and steadfastly held to that position for several stressful weeks. I have striven ever since to prove her initial impressions incorrect. Count this as another try.

★ CONTENTS ★

★ PHOTOS ★

★ PREFACE ★

AN EXAMPLE HELPS ANCHOR A PRINCIPLE in your mind. Jesus and his followers used parables. Harvard and this book use case studies. Now, the difference between a moral principle and leadership is that while Jesus could talk about moral red lines, you will search a long way for similar leadership absolutes. Particular principles work when mixed with specific personalities and situations. If you only want to be an excellent manager, do so; there is great challenge in that calling. If you truly want to be a leader, however, you need to understand your own abilities as well as leadership techniques.

I have two cautions if you choose the leadership track. The first is that leadership is highly personalized. Don't blindly adopt the successful methods of others. No matter how successful they were or might be, their leadership style is blended to their personality. We are all unique. The chances are overwhelming that another's approach will not serve you well. We learn in very different ways. We have disparate skills. Secondly, not all problems will yield to a "one-hammer" solution, no matter how good you become at wielding that tool. One knock-them-dead ability will not be sufficient. You will face too many diverse problems. You need to develop a range of methods (many call these "tools") compatible with your own personality. Then practice, practice, practice. Add to your skills as you gain experience.

There are also two practical guides. Never choose a tool so distant from your basic personality that it makes you uncomfortable. In other words, if you need empathy to make a practice work, and personal rapport is not one of your strengths, select a different approach. Or, if you are an introvert at heart, it is a mistake to choose a method only an extrovert could love. Second, once you have selected a tool, find an immediate way to practice. You will never enjoy success with an unfamiliar tool, any more than you can pick up Rory McIlroy's 2-iron, take one swing, and expect your ball to stick on the green.

As a golfer needs his or her own clubs, in leadership you need to make your own decisions. In this book I will describe what I tried myself. I will portray what worked for me and where I believe I erred. You can gauge my personality, judge how it might differ from yours, and compute your own windage adjustments. Of course, since this is a leadership book, you are expected to do some thinking for yourself. Begin by personally evaluating these vignettes. Were there less risky approaches available? I know this may be the case. Finally, if a similar situation drives you to gird your own loins, will you be adequately prepared?

I remind the reader that I believe all leadership is personal and I recommend that readers select only the level of risk with which they are personally comfortable. My comfort level was driven by my own personal experiences. I believe I owe the reader a succinct explanatory note.

Seminal events in our lives are often much more easily identifiable in retrospect. I was an excellent high school student. My father pushed me into wrestling to help me deal with a challenging high school physical environment. The consequential toughness was exactly what the Naval Academy selection committee was looking for. They had lots of exemplary student applicants, but not enough wrestlers. Several years later I was interviewed for nine hours by Adm. Hyman Rickover's deputy before being assigned to a submarine that had once been the pride of the fleet. What he knew and I didn't was that there was trouble brewing. The ship in question had been run hard and put away wet for fifteen years.

These problems had been dealt with previously by manning the ship with superstars, but now there was a pell-mell submarine-building program under way and insufficient superstars to go around. The maintenance IOUs that had been piling up on the forecastle were all past due. I was sent there to stem the tide. The next three years would be an extraordinary period in my life, not least of all because I would discover that many of the ship's electrical components, including the hundreds of miles of wiring that made the ship work, were teetering on the edge of bursting into flames.

A fire at sea in a submarine is a challenge. There is no place to flee. Topside, the deck of a submarine is unsafe. Down below, the crew and the fire are consuming the same oxygen. The problem has to be attacked immediately. I called fires "bears." Either we killed the bear or the bear ate us. In the three years I was engineer officer on board that ship, we had more than a thousand fires—more than one a day—as we

hurriedly replaced every inch of wire and nearly every electrical component. Some blazes involved a quarter of the ship. One burned for so
long CBS television spied the smoke and reported the ship lost at sea.
Most fires were thankfully smaller. But all were life-threatening. I was
in charge of fighting each and every fire. I couldn't ever fail. If I had not
been a leader before, I became one to survive. I learned myriad lessons
and looked risk dead in the eyes. I was still in my twenties.

★ ACKNOWLEDGMENTS ★

A NUMBER OF PEOPLE HAVE READ various drafts of this manuscript. Among the most insightful comments I received were those from Marv Langston, a longtime friend possibly best known for his service as the Defense Department's first chief information officer. Perceptiveness may be a characteristic of men in this business as Art House, the chief cybersecurity risk officer for the state of Connecticut, also provided particularly helpful advice. Adm. John Jolliffe, himself a unique leader, also provided keen insight. John Odegaard, who was at the time the CEO of the Naval War College Foundation, was of great assistance in helping me reconstruct details from our years of service together in the Pacific. Former secretary of defense Bill Perry's reading of the case study dealing with Project Sapphire was invaluable. I also appreciated the late Dr. Todd Kauderer's expert advice on naval war gaming, just as I always appreciated the sound guidance of his father, Vice Adm. Bud Kauderer.

I talked other people into reading one or more cases. They included Nada Alsouze, Paul (Jerry) Bremer, Nancy Bithell, Irene Bithell, Tom Bithell, Walt Bithell, Jay Davis, Eric Dwoskin, Joe Dyer, Kent Ewing, Aaron Johnson, Dave Goebel, Jim Hogg, Mike Hough, Bill Houley, Bud Kauderer, Pat Kennedy, Pam Lenehan, Bill McDaniels, Vago Muradian, Ginger Oliver, Tim Oliver, John Petersen, Ralph Schlichter, Mac Williams, Leslie Zimring, Michael Zimring, and Ann Zumwalt. I valued each comment they offered.

PART 1

Personal Traits a Leader Should Strive to Strengthen

1 ★ MY SHADOW

CRITICAL MOMENTS NEED TO BE RECOGNIZED. Like the Supreme Court justice who couldn't describe pornography but recognized it when he saw it, a leader knows a critical moment when he or she sees it. In such cases you simply must act.

I have many flaws. Years of competition have taught me what they are. As a consequence, I long ago adopted an imaginary soul much like me, but with none of my fears and failings. Over time that presence has become a shadow in my mind. My shadow never stumbles. He is articulate. My shadow never hesitates. My shadow knows no fear. My shadow helps me lead myself.

My shadow doesn't appear during my usual days. He doesn't bother me when I am spending time with my family. His indistinct form only silently begins to form when a challenge begins to force me outside my comfort zone.

This case study dates to the end of the Cold War and its immediate aftermath. There were about 60,000 nuclear weapons in the world (nearly all belonging to the United States or the Soviet Union). I had worked with these special devices. I appreciated the potential terrible threat posed by the poisonous raw plutonium in their warheads as well as their explosive power. It was important that both Russia and the United States, as the leaders of the two alliances, have a fail-proof control system for keeping track of the more mobile weapons. Before the Iron Curtain fell, we both assumed the best of each other.

On December 3, 1989, President George H. W. Bush met with Soviet leader Mikhail Gorbachev on board the Soviet cruise liner *Maxim Gorky* off Malta. The Cold War was over. The United States had won! As soon as Americans had consumed a congratulatory beer or two, many who had studied the Soviet Union immediately began worrying. Nearly every economist predicted Russia would go through a downturn. In the interim, without their internal draconian emphasis on defense, what was the incentive for the Russians to keep track of the 37,000 nuclear weapons that were now principally economic burdens to them?

Most of the devices were mobile. Only a few thousand were the enormous transcontinental ones that required a major evolution to move. And many were located in Kazakhstan, a satellite republic the Soviets had abused for years. After the dissolution, would the Russians still keep adequate track of their nuclear weapons—even those not in Russia—or would the world suffer from tragedy due to a "loose nuke"? The Soviet Union was literally tearing itself apart before our eyes. Great headlines if you had worried for decades about the world balance of power. Not such good news if you were concerned about those 37,000 nuclear weapons.

Kazakhstan, the largest Soviet republic, the one physically located between Russia and China, the one where Russia's space station was controlled, the one with most of the Soviet gold and oil assets, declared sovereignty in late 1990. The following summer, a failed coup attempt weakened Gorbachev while Russian Federation president Boris Yeltsin emerged a hero. The latter was reportedly pressing to reconstitute the Soviet Union. Before he could, all the former Soviet republics rushed for the door. On December 16, 1991, Kazakhstan became the last Soviet republic to leave the USSR.

The new state instantly became a poster child for instability. Kazakhstan had the longest border in the world with both Russia and China. It had no effective military, and ethnic Russians made up nearly 37 percent of the Kazakh population. In addition, Russia had hundreds of armored regiments within three days' march of the Kazakh capital of Almaty.

If it were possible to be even more concerned about uncontrolled nuclear weapons, these events clicked tensions another level higher in the Pentagon. In Kazakhstan, the local politicians involved were much closer to the fire, and they knew at least one related dark secret the Russians didn't even want mentioned. I am sure Nursultan Nazarbayev, president of Kazakhstan, and his trusted staff watched Moscow, especially Mr. Yeltsin, very carefully. Finally, one evening . . .

I had gone to bed to the gentle sound of snow building on the window panes in our home in northern Virginia. Our ringing phone startled me awake just after midnight. I picked the receiver up quickly to hear, "Dave, do you want a hundred nuclear weapons and a ton of plutonium?"

The voice at the other end was not a native English speaker. English was possibly not even her second language. She had a soft tone that was centered in the frequencies I had the most difficulty hearing, but my memory was dinging to remind me I had spoken to her before. A ton of plutonium! A hundred nuclear weapons! Maybe we had talked a year ago. Maybe more. What had been the occasion? It didn't matter. Processed plutonium is a deadly poison that spreads more easily than talcum powder. There was only one right answer. "Of course."

Who was this?

"Can you get to Georgetown in half an hour? We have been in town for four days. We can't get anyone to listen!"

My mental Rolodex was still clicking over. Suddenly it stopped on a specific card. I hadn't seen the woman for two long years. Dr. Thue Van Le had been the owner of a shipping business on the West Coast. She ran a company large enough to earn her a senior role in the California Republican Party during at least some of the Reagan years.

Her voice was rising. "None of my senators would even meet with us! You are my last chance! They must leave tomorrow!"

Who must? Dr. Van Le was a political heavy hitter. There had to be a reason she couldn't get attention in Washington and why senior politicians were running the other way.

I found myself out of bed standing at the window looking at the falling snow. I checked with my shadow. He was sitting in the corner of the bedroom. We kept an orange-covered cloth chair there that my spouse had used during both her pregnancies. His stern look reminded me that loose nukes were a real problem. I asked Dr. Van Le for the address. My spouse was still sound asleep.

I hurriedly dressed and drove off into the snow to what appeared to be a deserted copy shop in Georgetown. The street was unlit. When I knocked on the store door, it wasn't latched. The metal-framed dark glass swung open at my touch. Two men with shotguns invited me in. They motioned me through an x-ray scanner (this was no copy shop!) and into an elevator that led to the second floor. Suddenly it was as if I were in an exquisite hotel in Hong Kong, complete with tapestries, porcelain, and thick wool rugs.

I later found out I had entered a Chinese "safe" house, a secure location constructed completely inside what on the outside looked like a slightly run-down office building. The Chinese government had turned out their red carpet for this event. I'm not sure whether the thick wool rugs or the shotguns should have been my first indication that I was about to meet with someone very important.

After a three-hour breakfast with a man who represented himself as the president of Kazakhstan, I left. My host was offering nuclear weapons and either plutonium or highly enriched uranium in exchange for visible American support. He hoped that would keep President Yeltsin from reclaiming his country. I was convinced he was sincere, and the offer appeared to be in America's best interests. I believed that facilitating this would be the most significant professional act I could ever accomplish.

I also now understood why politicians were running the other way. If the offer was true, it was going to break some china! My Kazakh breakfast host had told me the Soviets had bamboozled us! By knowing the highly classified limitations of our high-technology Keyhole low-earth-orbit observation satellites, as well as the satellite revisit times to the Soviet missile fields, they had assembled a confusing display of huge cranes and high-wheeled trucks. The Soviets had then staged one of the world's largest magic disappearing acts during a scheduled missile replacement!

The result had been a successful smuggling of more than a hundred city-busting nuclear weapons from under the noses of our American satellites to a Kazakh mountain cave. This had been a clear violation of President Nixon and Henry Kissinger's keystone achievement of the Strategic Arms Limitation Agreement (SALT 1). It was all ancient history now.

The very existence of these weapons, however, touched on two inside-the-Beltway sensitivities. Control of the weapons had probably been lost because the CIA underestimated the damage done by a spy (William Kampiles) within their midst. But Kampiles was only a minor player in the legion of American turncoats that had recently been exposed: Aldrich Ames also from the CIA, Jonathan Pollard and the Walker family from the Navy, the NSA's Ronald Pelton, Robert Hanssen from the FBI, etc. The United States looking foolish and moles in our intelligence agencies—neither was a popular topic of conversation.

But the Kazakh's story made sense to me. I had previously had to do my own damage control in submarines to deal with the Walker brothers' espionage long before they were arrested, and I personally knew Soviet spy craft had been top notch. Nevertheless, how was I going to convince anyone that Kazakhstan was a legitimate opportunity? The

Kazakh president had given me his calling card, but anyone with a bad accent and a hand-printing press could have engraved calling cards.

President Nazarbayev had complained that senators had refused to meet with him during the previous week even although he had been accompanied by someone (Dr. Van Le) with impeccable political credentials. Without some sort of proof, the story was tantalizing—oil, gold, plutonium, hidden nuclear weapons not included in the strategic arms limitation agreement—but! I checked on my shadow: still there and encouraging action.

It was also still dark and snowing. I drove carefully out to the CIA headquarters at Langley. There was little traffic at that hour. DC closes down when it snows.

I knew my friend Rich Haver came in early. He and I had a long professional history and Rich was now the number three or four at the agency. I waited alongside the road leading to the headquarters for an hour, stamping my feet in the snow to stay warm until I recognized Rich's car. I waved at him to pull over. As I had gotten up from the safe house breakfast table, I had slipped our breakfast salt and pepper shakers into my jacket pocket. I gave Rich my souvenirs, now in a plastic bag from my car's glove compartment, along with a request to identify any prints the analysts could find. I had decided it would be better if Rich wasn't hampered by any story to go with my request, and he, good friend that he was, didn't insist.

Next it was down Route 123 and to the Pentagon, first to the Navy intelligence center to check up on the latest news from Kazakhstan. The watch officer reinforced what the Kazakh president had told me hours earlier. There was ongoing unrest and fresh riots in Almaty. Nazarbayev had told me he needed to get back and quell the tension. Unless President Nazarbayev met President Clinton before the last flight to Europe out of Dulles this afternoon, a golden opportunity was going to be missed, perhaps forever. I had about six hours to make something happen.

At 6 a.m. I was camped at the door of the director of the Defense Intelligence Agency waiting for the man in charge to arrive. Intelligence chiefs always get in early. This would be the easiest approach. He was from a different service but I was more than willing for the DIA director to take the credit for bringing the president of Kazakhstan and the president of the United States together.

It quickly became apparent, though, that the director was not only uninterested, he was antagonistic! By 6:15 he had finished telling me how stupid he thought I was. Neither he nor his predecessors had ever lost control of any nukes, they had done a careful review of the Kampiles situation and none of the turncoat spies at the CIA had done any real damage to defense programs, there were no "loose nukes" or loose highly enriched uranium in Kazakhstan, and President Nazarbayev was back at home in his capital of Almaty. The director told me I was to keep any different thoughts to myself if I understood "what was good for me."

At 6:30 a.m. I was back in the friendlier confines of the Navy portion of the Pentagon and sitting in the Vice Chief of Naval Operations' office. The vice chief was a four-star. I knew him well and obviously we were both in the same service. He listened patiently but was also disapproving. "Dave, don't take this anywhere else. There is nothing there. Given the unrest in the former Soviet world, there are frauds everywhere pushing stories about loose nukes. Forget about this."

Not exactly what I believed to be correct. Back to the more hostile parts of the Pentagon. At 8 a.m. I was speaking to the chairman of the Joint Chiefs of Staff. "Dave, one of my office's jobs is to track those weapons. If what your source is saying is true, it means that one of my predecessors screwed up. I don't believe that. We are not going to go any further on this. You are going to drop it."

I went back to my office, cancelled all my morning meetings and got myself a cup of coffee. Despite several direct orders to let it go, I had taken this issue all the way to the top in the military. I wore a uniform. I was at the end of the road. I was also at a practical Washington time barrier. Even if heaven and earth could be rearranged, if nothing happened before noon there would be insufficient time to put together a meeting between the two presidents. The White House day would no longer have sufficient minutes left. I got another cup of coffee and wandered around watching my staff work. I could tell by the way their shoulders were flexing that I was driving them nuts. I decided to leave the office and take a stroll.

In the winter in the Pentagon, especially when it is snowing, the best place to walk is around the E ring. The corridors are wide and the walk is almost a mile if you religiously stick to the outer edge. My shadow followed me. The Navy offices are on the fourth floor. After my first complete circuit, I took one of the many sets of stairs that dropped down a level. After my second trip around I stopped opposite the secretary of defense's office. Bill Perry had moved up from his job as the Pentagon deputy and was now the secretary of defense. I knew Secretary Perry from his previous service on Navy advisory boards. He was a hands-on decision maker. Over the past year, in the event I ever needed access to him, I had taken the reasonable precaution of bringing flowers to his administrative assistant on appropriate occasions. I stuck my head in her office door: "May I speak to the secretary for five minutes?"

"Let me check, Dave. I think he has a free moment right now."

I got two sentences into the story of my early morning when Secretary Perry stopped me. He called for his four key advisors and suggested we both get fresh coffee while we waited for them to assemble. When they arrived, he had me relate what had happened. His staff argued for about an hour. I was not winning. I think the secretary was ready to side with his staff when his administrative assistant slid into the room. She whispered something in his ear.

Bill Perry held up his hand to halt the discussion and announced he had a call from Jim Woolsey, the director of the CIA. The secretary then told Director Woolsey he was putting the latter on speakerphone.

"Bill, how the hell did Dave Oliver get Nursultan Nazarbayev's fingerprints?"

The secretary stood up, excused us all, and said it was time for him to take a trip across the Potomac River to speak to the president. I and the others returned to our day jobs.

When I got home that night, my spouse asked where I had disappeared to that snowy morning. I suspected that the whole situation was now classified and lamely said, "I had some things I needed to work on." She nodded, and from her frosty look I knew she believed I was omitting a few details. "Well, the secretary of defense, Bill Perry, called a few minutes before you got home. He asked me to give you a message. 'Tell Dave the president talked to your friends and decided to do it.'"

Under the label of Project Sapphire, Russia destroyed the previously hidden nuclear weapons, and the radioactive material from Kazakhstan was flown to the Oak Ridge National Laboratory in Tennessee for initial processing and then on to a Canadian reactor that could "burn"

Secretary of Defense Bill Perry. Project Sapphire, in which he dramatically reduced the number of nuclear weapons in the world, was only one of his extraordinary accomplishments. *Department of Defense*

the isotope to manufacture electricity. The ex-Soviet material thus provided years of power to the Detroit and Toronto areas. In the process, Kazakhstan joined South Africa and Ukraine as the only countries in the world to voluntarily give up their nuclear weapons, a swords-into-plowshares success story.

When life gets particularly vexing, before you quit, check with your shadow. The individual most frequently needing leadership is you.

2 ★ YOM KIPPUR

SOMETIMES LEADERS MUST color outside the lines.

In 1973 I was working for Adm. Bud Zumwalt, who was then the Chief of Naval Operations, the most senior officer in the Navy, an office commonly abbreviated as the CNO. At that time, the CNO still directed most worldwide Navy warfare operations. I was possibly the most junior person on his staff, or at least the youngest from one of the three primary warfare areas of air, surface, and submarines. I thus became the go-to bloke for some of his more impossible taskings: "Go tell the submariners and Admiral Rickover to cut the approved budget for the ballistic missile submarine program by a billion dollars; if they won't, you do it!" I also picked up the improbable jobs—"develop a prioritized list of every research program in the Navy, then recommend what we need to fund first"—as well as the more unattainable goals, such as "We need to bring the North Vietnamese to the bargaining table. Give me a plan to provide to President Nixon."

When you are young you cannot imagine failure, so it was all great fun! In between the significant challenges there were always the routine activities inherent in my role as the most junior person on the staff. This case study refers to one of those dog-walking details.

One September day, Admiral Zumwalt called me in to his office. He told me the Navy laboratory system had developed a recent modification in the infrared seeker for the Navy's (and Air Force's) main short-range airplane air-to-air missile. This missile was the famous AIM-9, commonly known as the Sidewinder. I was familiar with the missile and its unusual history. It had been invented by Dr. Bill McLean, surreptitiously against the Navy's initial objections, on the bench in McLean's own garage at China Lake. It had subsequently become the most effective air-to-air short-range weapon in our arsenal and was currently being used by every service, even the Air Force, for aerial dogfights! Dr. McLean was now running the Navy's entire China Lake Naval Air Weapons Station in the western Mojave Desert region of California and was constantly upgrading the AIM-9 missile.

As I stood at attention in his office, Zumwalt added that the researchers believed this recent change to the AIM-9 was significant. Physically, we were only talking about two wires connecting some new circuitry logic not much larger than a half dollar that enhanced the infrared guidance of the missile. It was the twelfth such incremental improvement in the missile, so it would be known as the Lima mod. I nodded. I knew there had to be something special about this; usually the CNO didn't waste many words on me. Normally he just used his bushy eyebrows to soundlessly start me moving in some direction out of the room. As he continued, I gathered that there were 1,050 of these test articles in a cardboard box down the hall. They currently were residing in the office of the vice admiral who ran the Navy's research efforts. The CNO directed me to deliver that box to an address in downtown DC.

Within an hour, I was on my way. I knew my destination was a particularly tough area, a slum near what is now the left field exit of the Nationals' baseball park. But it would be daylight, I was in civilian clothes (officers assigned to the Pentagon during those post–Pentagon Papers years normally did not wear a uniform in order to avoid physical altercations with antiwar protesters), I was physically in good shape, and someone else would be there. I was slightly worried about the box because it was an awkward size and required both hands to handle.

I exited the executive sedan at the right address, picked my box up off the cracked and grassy sidewalk, and looked around as the car drove off. There were no houses on the street, just empty lots and boarded-up buildings. And as I began to wonder where exactly my meeting was supposed to take place, everything went dark and a hard piece of metal was thrust into my spine. The box whooshed out of my hands and someone calmly spoke into my right ear. "Just stand here and count slowly to fifty before you remove the bag from over your head."

And when I did so, I was alone. The only person on the entire block was an elderly lady a hundred yards away. She was pushing a battered grocery cart into an alley.

I walked in the direction of the Marine barracks at 8th & I until I could hail a cab. Then I immediately returned to the Pentagon. There I immediately knocked on the CNO's door to report what had happened. I interrupted him writing. I don't recall my exact words. I may have been stressed. He merely nodded, said "very well," and returned his attention to the paperwork on his desk.

Very well? What the hell? I had lost those super-special things! But he was now ignoring me, so I slipped out of his office. It was not the first time I had not understood the workings of Admiral Zumwalt's mind.

Now I had a choice. According to the Pentagon organizational chart I actually had two other bosses, Capt. Kin McKee and Capt. Paul Gillcrist. They would both later become admirals. I had been in a rush earlier to do what the CNO had directed and I hadn't mentioned my tasking to either, a possible faux pas. Should I now make amends by sharing the disastrous results? I decided to select door number three. I awarded myself early liberty and headed home for a warm bowl of soup.

Ten days later, on October 6, 1973, in what became known as the Yom Kippur War, a coalition of Arab states, led by Egypt and Syria, invaded Israel. After two and a half weeks of hard fighting, Israel achieved a military victory.

At the time Linda and I were living in Arlington, Virginia, in a house the first floor of which was about six feet above grade. This arrangement lifted us clear of the snows that frequently descended. Concrete steps and simple black iron railings led up from the sidewalk to our front door. One early morning as I prepared to go to work, I could not get our front storm door open. I pushed and pushed to no avail. Finally, I went out the back door and walked around the house to eye the obstruction. Standing in our front lawn, I could see the obvious reason. A bulging woven basket on the front stoop was pressed against the door. The heavy basket was overflowing with bottles of wine.

The wines were all native Israeli. There was no card.

Prior to the Yom Kippur War, Congress had taken the position that any American department or agency wishing to export arms to Israel would have to balance those with equivalent exports to Arab nations. The president's national security advisor, Dr. Henry Kissinger, had emphasized a similar position for the administration. Those actions by two-thirds of our government had essentially halted America's normally robust arms support for Israel.

History reports that when Syria and Egypt attacked Israel, both America and Israel were caught by surprise. I have my reasons to suspect that "history" may have this wrong. Dr. Kissinger may have been surprised. And thus so may have been President Richard Nixon. But I am not sure Israel was caught by surprise. And, I am fairly sure, Adm. Bud Zumwalt was not. I always have mentally drawn a few looping lines between the following:

- Based on other errands I ran for Admiral Zumwalt, I suspected he was not overly fond of Dr. Kissinger.
- I never checked to see what was inside the box taken from me on September 27, 1973. Of course, it may have been cornflakes. Something was inside. The box rattled.
- Common wisdom as I write these words in 2020 is that the AIM-9L was in full production by 1977 and that the first use of the Sidewinder 9L in combat occurred during the Gulf of Sidra (1981) engagement and again during the Falklands War (1982). During both these engagements an eightfold improvement in kill rate was observed. Interestingly, when Syria and Egypt attacked Israel in 1973, the two Arab nations lost 172 aircraft and Israel reportedly lost only 20.
- On March 12, 2018, on the occasion of Israel's seventieth anniversary, Adm. Bud Zumwalt was recognized by the Israeli embassy in Washington and the Jewish News Syndicate as one of the seventy greatest American contributors to the U.S.-Israel relationship.
- Back in November and December 1973, my spouse and her guests found the wines from our front stoop to be uniformly excellent.

Leadership is not all roses, chocolates, formal dinners with interesting people, or obvious courses of action. Sometimes senior leaders have to make their own personal decisions on a situation that may go either way. A good leader has a plan for damage control, often a closely held plan. As the adage advises, loose lips can sink ships.

3 ★ MIRRORS

EXTRAORDINARILY SUCCESSFUL PEOPLE often devote a long time in one-on-one sessions evaluating and counseling their subordinates. But these leaders are the exceptions. Instead, young superstars are too often recruited with alacrity and discarded with apathy.

The good leader realizes that all new employees, as well as old hands in new jobs, don't have stable professional images. The boss is their mirror. Good bosses reflect the performances they want to see. Good leaders also keep their own image polished.

Want an example? Think back to your last county fair. It was probably early fall. Green monster harvesting machines were still sweeping the last fields. Some friends' son or daughter was running pell-mell for the 4-H barn. I love fairs. I particularly enjoy the midway. The smell of sugar in the air. Shuffling your feet through the shredded corncobs. Distinctive sounds you only hear once a year: the cry of barkers, the whine of spinning steel cages, the shrieking teenagers, the low thump of baseballs against canvas, sharp cracks from the rifle booth. The carnival is a center of the unexpected. Its shadowy tension is part of the charm. A little misdirection here, a feint or two there, a momentary sparkle that flashes in the corner of your eye.

Some of the events are eerily real. Your dimes freely skip through dishes that look a lot like the ones on Aunt Maude's Thanksgiving table! The bumper cars remind you of driving in Boston. But other aspects are purely freaky! For one, think back to that scary house of mirrors.

Well, perhaps it was scary to children, but how many big people did you see lined up at the house of mirrors ticket booth? Adults do everything else at a carnival; they even eat cotton candy, and barf when they get off the roller coasters. Why don't they walk through the house of mirrors? Because, for adults, a house of mirrors is bor-r-r-ring. Adults know their own image. There is no Hogwarts School of Witchcraft and Wizardry magic available to them. They can no longer suspend disbelief. They may perhaps be childlike in other ways, but they know their own flaws and foibles. Adults immediately reject, without conscious thought, the "evidence" of outlandish appearance a concave or convex pane of silvered glass pretends to offer.

On the other hand, the young employee beginning a career, a new job, or even a new task has no such reference. With respect to the key concept of whether or not he or she is doing a good job, the new individual is working in a house of mirrors. A new person is unable to summarily reject and discard false "evidence." A new person needs and longs for true reflections daily. If a person's boss or coworkers indicate he or she isn't doing adequate work, even if those comments are completely false, some young people will accept that false judgment. They have no better frame of reference.

As a consequence, a young worker may find himself or herself turning from one crazy mirror to the next with no friend alongside to laugh the fears away. Is this any way for an organization to treat the "seed corn of its success"? What do you do to ensure one of your prized recruits doesn't inadvertently wander into your organization's crazy house?

I recommend three steps: spend significantly more time talking meaningfully with those who report to you, use (nearly only) positive feedback, and listen attentively for subtle messages.

I was once a young officer working in a particular submarine. Great deeds had been accomplished on board this ship and the vessel had a wonderful reputation. At the same time, the ship was certainly not what she once had been. There were 15 officers and 120 enlisted men assigned. In the two years I was on board, three times the normal complement of officers were rotated through that one ship. Thirty quit or were fired!

Now I will admit that I didn't ever do the math to prove that thirty out of thirty is statistically significant. But to be assigned to that submarine, each of these young men had to have been about Phi Beta Kappa (roughly the top 10 percent of their college class) and subsequently had to have graduated from a demanding eighteen-month technical program, one that significantly whittled away at their numbers. The ones that made it through were definitely competent enough to do the work assigned. They also had to be very motivated. Then why did these young men give up?

For years I wondered. For a long time, I thought that chance must have simply bunched a large number of losers in one particular place.

If I seem bitter, you should appreciate that each time one of the thirty left, I was assigned to pick up the departee's work in addition to my own. Each man made his own individual decision to quit, didn't he? Ipso facto, *quod erat demonstrandum*, or whatever it was my geometry teacher used to say.

In a later assignment, I worked on a different ship where thirteen out of eighteen people resigned or were fired and in still another where we lost seven of our nine young executives. In each of these places I was still working long hours with my head down. I still didn't catch on. As the years passed, however, and by chance I ran into many of the individuals who had quit (or been fired before they could decide to quit), I could not help but notice that nearly every one of these ex-shipmates had established impressive careers in challenging but different fields outside the Navy.

And then I was reading about how Dr. W. Edwards Deming, author and management consultant, viewed individual performance evaluations. Since Deming was a key individual in the rise of Japanese industry after World War II as well as in the nearly single-handed rescue of the U.S. automobile industry in the 1980s, I was prepped by his reputation to pay attention to his opinions.

When I personally spoke to him, Deming recommended that any performance discussion with employees be at least four hours in length!

How interesting. I know another who believed that four hours was the minimum time a supervisor should spend monitoring the performance of a workplace. That person was Adm. Hyman G. Rickover, the "Father of the Nuclear Navy." When I realized two of my mentors agreed, I decided I should change my approach for my direct reports. What were the results? Interesting. Very interesting.

The first fifteen minutes or half hour of each discussion was rough. No matter how often I did this, I felt that both of us were initially wondering how in the world we were going to stay in the same room for four hours without falling asleep or insulting one another. We were struggling to find a line of mutual interest.

But sometime between "good morning" and the ninety-minute mark, we always discovered some job-related item we both found worth talking about. Since I had already blocked off the entire morning for this one person, I found myself actually listening to my employee, if for no other reason so that I might segue to the items I had previously written on my three-by-five card. Whatever the reason, I actually paid attention. Therefore, I frequently picked up on nuances my conversation partner casually threw down that otherwise might have rolled unseen under the couch.

At the same time, my key employees, during the previous weeks when they realized they were going to have to spend a whole morning with me, spent some time thinking about what they wanted to say. Sometime after the first thirty minutes of getting comfortable, they began to get around to the things they didn't like about the way the organization was operating, the way I was doing my job, or whatever else was sticking in their craw. If they didn't have their own comments or opinions, they would share ones they had overheard from their coworkers. Four hours was long enough for them to dump what they had gathered from their entire social network.

My responsibility after the first half-hour or so often didn't involve much more than being a good recorder. Simply by being attentive, I obtained, in exchange for three of four hours of my time, an invaluable perspective on our organization. After I had done this for a year, I did my own self-evaluation of my process. And I was shocked!

In retrospect, nearly every one of my direct reports, even the extraordinary performers, was unsure of whether or not they were doing good work!

At the time, I was operating a multibillion-dollar organization, and I would have wagered a significant sum of my own money that I spoke to every single one of our key headquarters people every day. I would have bet almost that sum that I talked to nearly every employee, key or not, weekly in the normal course of my routine "walk arounds." I prided myself on providing positive feedback. But what I was doing was obviously inadequate! Which led me to thinking about carnivals and the house of mirrors.

Why should it surprise me that my key people weren't sure how they were doing? They were all positioned near the top of a large organization in a vibrant and competitive industry. The marketplace demanded innovation. Their promotion and compensation were based on how quickly each adapted. If their own private and family lives were anything like mine, they were also facing daily challenges as children made life decisions and other family members experienced life's vicissitudes. My people were essentially facing a brand new job every day. Yet they were experienced enough to know their coworkers didn't know any more than they. So everyone was counting on me to tell them how well they were doing. I was their one true mirror.

If you are a leader, you are the one person everyone looks up to. They believe what you say, whether that conversation is formal or a glancing frown or quick smile. Just like a child in a hall of carnival mirrors, many of your people don't have stable professional images. If you tell them they are only four feet tall, even if all the objective evidence says five-foot-nine, some part of them is going to fear their growth may well be stunted.

I now understand, so many years later, how so many good young men could have quit or failed (recall my earlier thirty out of thirty, thirteen of eighteen, and seven of nine examples). At the time, we had a string of leaders in our organization who devoted their time to criticizing the help. I cannot tell you how often I heard a supervisor tell someone, "You didn't adequately support me!" or "If you had only thought ahead!," as those "leaders" sucked up every smidgen of praise that rolled down the corporate ladder and simultaneously attempted to unload responsibility for every real or imagined failure. These "leaders" did not understand their role as mirrors.

Good leaders reflect the performance they want to see.

4 ★ ASK TWICE

A LEADER HAS TO UNDERSTAND human behavior. He needs to influence people. It is thus worth spending time understanding individual and group behavior, not only what you hope it to be, but recognizing what it is.

One of the specific problems with us humans is that many of us have an initial inclination to lie when we are unsure or feel like we might be in trouble. No matter how much training we do to the contrary, people often don't offer up the whole truth. If you expect unvarnished facts to freely flow at first blush, you are going to find yourself making decisions based on bad data. My mother's old complaint often rings in memory's ear: "Why do you always ask the same question twice?" Because I want to know the truth.

This is a disappointing fact to harp on, especially to military people who have spent years emphasizing the importance of making accurate and complete initial reports. Nevertheless, military history is chock-full of critical errors based on lies, such as when the United States went to war in Vietnam after the USS *Turner Joy* (DD 951) reported being fired upon by North Vietnamese ships in the Gulf of Tonkin on August 4, 1964. It was a while ago, but that war went on for nearly a decade, 58,220 Americans were killed in action, and yet the actual event never occurred. It existed only in the minds and fears of some of the officers and crew of the *Turner Joy*.

This same principle holds in lesser situations than one that initiated the longest active war of our history. I can literally think of dozens of examples, but let me give you one that doesn't revolve around an international incident. Once upon a time I was conducting an investigation in which we suspected command discipline had broken down. No one could quite put a label on what was wrong, but few things in that organization ran smoothly. This group of professionals acted like six-year-olds at a neighborhood soccer practice. None of them were doing their jobs and they were all running after the same moving object!

When a situation is that rotten it is often difficult to fix. The secondary rot can obscure the original failure. I have always found the best approach is to simply select one egregious incident and trace the flaw back to the original fault. If the lead peters out, don't worry, in situations like this there will always be another thread to follow. The story, like the scene in a thousand-piece jigsaw puzzle, will eventually be exposed.

In this particular case there had been problems bubbling around the San Diego submarine base for quite a while. The last infamous incident had been a raging fire that had nearly blown apart the Ballast Point ammunition dump. The blaze had begun when a two-ton submarine torpedo rolled off its transportation cradle and tumbled down the face of a sheer two-hundred-foot cliff. The weapon exploded right where it was definitely not wanted: in the storage area for submarine high explosives carved into the hills below. I had been on patrol in my submarine when the fire took place, but reportedly the flames had been quite impressive!

Subsequently, an investigation had been conducted, with the usual questions included: Had sufficient firefighting training been performed? Was coordination with local officials adequate? Exactly how much delay had there been in permitting the town's fire engines into the fenced-off submarine base? There had also been some general carping as to who had been how brave (the award to one particular senior officer had been accompanied by sotto voce accusations of "grandstanding"). In the end the investigation had concluded undramatically that no one had been specifically at fault and recommended that an additional fire station be built on the perimeter of the high-explosive storage area. The necessary funds had been appropriated and that facility was currently under construction.

It was now a year later and I was in San Diego in charge of reviewing a new problem. This investigation had been initiated by a rash of abnormal events: excessive incidents of driving while intoxicated, excessive personnel turnover rate, and high sexual assault rates. It was obvious there was some relationship between all of these and alcohol, but the line on acceptable social drinking in the military has always been a bit fuzzy. At the time there was a war going on and these people were the frontline warriors for our country. Didn't they deserve some slack?

After two weeks I knew nada. Despite interviewing several hundred potential witnesses and obtaining sworn statements from each one, there was not one promising manila file in any of the gray cabinets that now lined my temporary office. The two attorneys assigned to me were not much help. I had followed several leads, but all of them had petered out. The drug problems in this area were relatively low. The local alcohol abuse plan seemed reasonable, if a bit laxly implemented. I had heard several different reports about last year's big fire. In fact, I had toured the entire base, including the weapons area isolated on the top of the base's tallest hill. I had even interviewed the sailor who had been driving the transportation vehicle when his brakes had failed the previous year on the steep slope coming down from the weapons station. He had told me that where the road sharply turned, he had nearly gone over the cliff along with the warshot. The driver's dive out of the open-topped cab at the turn had saved his life! Good thing he was young and agile or he probably would have broken his neck.

I was getting tired of chasing my own tail on the investigation. I also had a home and it wasn't in San Diego. My small staff was also weary. We had been doing this for fourteen straight days. They had lost track of whom we had interviewed and whom we had not. Which is what explained the screwup that led to the scheduling duplication. I was sitting in the unpainted office that had been provided us late one Saturday evening wondering if I should wrap this investigation up as a lost cause and try to make some excuse to my boss. Maybe I needed a week off. Or maybe my entire approach was wrong. Perhaps I would get further if I ignored any relationship with alcohol. Suddenly I realized my senior attorney was administering the oath to the same unlucky torpedo cart driver we had previously interviewed. I hadn't been paying attention when the latter walked in.

The sailor of course didn't realize he was only here by error. He thought we knew something!

Before I could tell him it was a mistake and he was excused, he was already nervously speaking very quickly, in a rural twang that identified him as coming from my own home state of Indiana, leaning forward sincerely, his forearms on his knees, addressing me from across the room.

"I been thinking about what you all asked me before. You know, I still remember about that fire. It sure was lucky no one got hurt real bad. Did you hear how close those damn flames got to setting off more of the f—n' weapons, excuse my French, sir? I was flat scared that day.

"You know I hadn't been drinking that much that afternoon. Not more than a six-pack. I mean I know what my AA guy tells me, but all the other weapons guys drink lots more than me. Hell, that's probably why the LT told me to drive the truck that afternoon when the sub had to have a warshot to get underway after those Russkies."

The green light on the recorder on the desk beside the attorney who had been administering the oath was steady and bright, the two reels were rolling, and the young sailor was doing his best to look deep into my eyes. He had been carrying this burden on his soul for more than a year. As the words quickly tumbled out, I knew he had repeated this story to himself lots of times late at night. Now he was going to pass his guilt on to me. "I only wish I hadn't taken that beer with me." His voice slowed an almost imperceptible measure. He paused. He knew he now had our full attention. There is a bit of the drama queen in all of us. "If I had put it down before I left the office, instead of setting it on the dash of the cab, it wouldn't have tipped when I turned down the hill. I was lucky to fall outta that cab at the curve when I reached to catch the beer."

He leaned back in his chair. He had waited over a year to tell someone the real story. "No guardrail on the road there. I might have gone over the cliff with that f—n' torpedo. OK if I smoke in here? Either of you got a ciggy?"

I left the attorneys to deal with notarizing the statement and immediately drove up the hill to the torpedo maintenance facility, a large building that was divided into two sections. The northern half was reserved for the "line" used to prepare the exercise torpedoes that would be fired for practice in the local operating area during the submarine exercises schedule during this coming week. The southern half, separated only by a connected series of small yellow stylized fish painted on the cement floor, held a separate series of working stations for the warshots that submarines would be taking on patrol against the Russians and Chinese. It was early afternoon. This time my visit wasn't expected. On the opposite side of the room from the front door, a metal trash can half full of ice and beer was sitting next to one of the work benches. The condensation ring on the sealed cement spread out four or five inches. The supervisor wasn't present. I took the opportunity to look through his room. In his closet there was an opened case of Jim Beam bourbon. The box was missing four quart bottles.

Once the cart driver gave us such a bright and shiny key, the puzzle of all the problems in the area was quickly solved. The torpedo maintenance supervisor was not the only senior drunk on the base. And since one of them was the base chief of staff, the staff security officer had been running a great little blackmail scheme. Within a few days I was able to correlate abnormalities that had previously seemed completely unrelated.

Was I brighter than the people who had done the initial (and a subsequent redo) fire investigations? Probably not. Definitely less organized. If we hadn't erred and scheduled one specific person to be interviewed twice, we might never have known what had happened. A whole bunch of senior people had certainly successfully lied to themselves and everyone else for a long, long time up to that point.

It is not obvious to the great majority of people why it is in their best interests to provide the truth, the whole truth, and nothing but the truth (often even when they are under oath) the first time asked. It is one thing to expect the whole truth from a trained senior military officer when a situation demands immediate action. Often a leader has to rely upon precisely that and I have done so.

But expecting every relevant fact to be offered up from everyone in the organization the first time they are asked, even when the facts as they understand them may not reflect well on themselves, is expecting a whole hell of a lot. How do you handle that? Let me give you another example. One time my chief of staff was investigating a possible case of sexual harassment. A relatively senior officer (junior to the chief of staff but very senior if you are a young enlisted or beginning officer) had been accused by two women of making unwanted sexual advances.

My chief of staff was having difficulty finding corroborating witnesses or evidence when a third woman's name kept coming up as a possible witness. The chief of staff interviewed her once and then again. She had an exceptional reputation and was well-respected throughout the organization. Many believed she was the most capable and professional officer in the command.

My chief of staff discussed his review with me. He was surprised the third woman had been relatively impatient with him, despite his relative seniority, in their interview session. She was serious about her career. She was not interested in wasting her time. She denied any sexual harassment had ever happened to her. She was not interested in any investigation.

The chief of staff had become convinced there was something behind the two women's stories. He called the third woman in for yet a third time and pressured her as best he could. She denied knowing about any harassment. He talked about her responsibility to other women who might not be as strong as she. He talked about her responsibility to the organization. He talked and talked . . .

She denied she knew anything. She finally simply stood up and walked out of his office.

An hour later she returned. She returned with an affidavit about the very abuse the suspect had forced upon her when he had cornered her one night two years earlier. The affidavit explicitly described the occasion in detail. After that episode, this composed young woman had immediately sat down and created a contemporaneous record, taken it to a commercial bank to be notarized, left a copy in her safety deposit box there, mailed a copy to her parents, and delivered the original to her supervisor in the chain of command. She had asked her immediate supervisor to prevent her from being harassed again and to have the offender reprimanded.

But nothing had been done to the offender. Instead, her immediate supervisor had been transferred later that week to an undesirable duty in the Middle East war zone (where he was killed in the line of duty). Shortly after her supervisor was sent away, she was transferred to a lesser billet in another organization, a difficult job to be promoted from. All this had happened a year previous to my assuming command over the entire organization.

Even if she assumed that people would believe her about the sexual assault, was it surprising she later avoided telling the truth the first time? Or the second time? The third? How could she be positive that I was so different from the last admiral? Sometime later after justice had finally been done, I apologized to her on behalf of the Navy. Based on our conversation, I was impressed with her. She was competent, organized, and generally had her act together, even if she was understandably past the point of forgiving and was intent upon leaving the Navy.

Critical initial reports from on-scene participants are sometimes later found to be completely wrong, skewed by personal or professional shortcomings and warped by adrenaline. The wise leader may not be expecting such inexactness, but he or she never discounts the possibility. If a decision is particularly important and the wind is beginning to rise, it is the wise leader that pauses and lets more information accumulate, gives people the opportunity to rethink and reconsider, and checks the facts while others are busy recommending precipitous action.

A leader must rely on the instincts that gained that leader his or her position. If a report doesn't resonate as pure and correct as a struck tuning fork, ask again.

5 ★ PREPARING TO BE RESPONSIBLE

ATHLETES WORK OUT FOR A REASON. Even the super jock must be confident in his or her own mind. Accidents and injuries happen more often when athletes operate outside their comfort spheres. Life is not different from sports in the need for preparation.

I was once on board a large repair tender, the USS *McKee* (AS 41), floating in a semiprotected harbor called Cold Bay. This faithfully named anchorage was in an out-of-the way location at the tip of the Alaskan panhandle, about midway between mainland Alaska and Russia. It was late fall. Snow was on the hills, ice was spider-webbing out each morning from the shore, and the Bering Sea was beginning to heave up to prepare the winter weather for North America. The tender was in this challenging place, along with a string of nuclear submarines that kept silently surfacing, coming alongside and later gliding away, as a Cold War exercise to demonstrate that submarines could be supported from places the Soviets never expected. Another tender team, lucky them, was performing the same sort of support work in Bali, Indonesia, where it was a tad warmer.

The USS *McKee* was more accustomed to operating in the balmy climes in and near San Diego, so the past several months had seen many preparations made to the ship, from checking out the topside rigging and the deicing plan to ensuring the ship's anchors and chains were prepared to hold against the expected seventy-knot gales. More critically, important training needed to be done with the helicopter team. Nearly every ship in the Navy is helicopter-capable to some degree. Most large surface ships have their own helicopter detachments that live on board. Some ships only have the ability to host a helicopter and its crew for short stays, while a few don't have the reinforced decks or even sufficient flat space to land these heavy metal birds. The *McKee* was one of the latter and was thus limited to having the aircraft hover above the ship while a load was hoisted up and down.

The thirteen hundred men and women doing submarine repair on board the *McKee* used a great deal of repair material, from steel plate to microchips, each and every day. Normally, while the *McKee* was firmly tied stern-end to a San Diego pier, the lack of a direct air logistics tie wasn't a problem. Trucks from the local airfields and railheads continuously unloaded pallets onto the pier alongside the ship. Loads were subsequently winched up and on board by the *McKee*'s many cranes. In the Aleutians there was an airhead nearby that would suffice to get daily resupplies in, but due to the shallow water at the available piers, the *McKee* would have to be anchored well out. The ship certainly had the cargo space to store several days of what it was projected to need, and it carried sufficient small boats on board to establish a ferry service to and from shore, but what if the seas were too rough for our boats for an extended period and we needed to urgently transport something off or on board the ship?

Good question. And the *McKee* had the ability to handle a helo, just not the deck strength to land one. But the process of air resupply is a delicate one that requires practice, practice, practice, and the utmost professionalism. It isn't something that can be done at the "good" level. A helo resupply is akin to the aerial performance at a circus. Every "catch" has to be perfect. The helo is moving, the quickly swiping blades are generating an electrical field, the ship is heaving with the sea. I have watched this particular circus from both sides: I have been on board the helo and also served in the landing zone. Both are high-adrenaline realms. Hovering in a helo in shifting winds above a pitching ship requires a pilot with superb hand-eye coordination. Dancing on a wet deck, atop a rolling ship while trying to trap the helo's lowering hoist with a grounded metal strap is an equally athletic endeavor. If you don't succeed, you are going to get severely shocked.

The metal cable carries an electrical charge (generated from electrons stripped from the air by the rapidly rotating blades) sufficient to knock your ass over the lifelines. Once that charge is grounded, the ship's team has to ignore the driving rain and wind while they guide the load down to the slippery deck, unhook and cleat it into place while the relative movement of the helo and the ship continually try to crush everyone or push them over the side. It has to be a well-choreographed dance between equally well-prepared partners. The flight deck CPO needs to know as much about the helicopter capability as the pilot. There were hand signals to learn, equipment to master, and teamwork to acquire. Each time an exercise was planned, several senior officers on the ship made it well-known that they were of the opinion that the time could better be spent on other preparations. But a Navy is not a democracy. The *McKee*'s commanding officer, Capt. Ralph Schlichter, had decided they were going to learn this tango.

In the months before we set course for Alaska, we made special arrangements to practice vertical replenishment every at sea period. I personally monitored the first set of exercises conducted in the flat, calm waters off San Diego. Each time subsequent exercises were scheduled there were the same complaints about possible dangers and other priorities. Yet the team got more proficient with every repetition.

A few months later, the USS *McKee* was riding at anchor in the harbor at Alaska. We had been there for a few weeks and the nearest town's hundred or so inhabitants, fishermen, a schoolteacher, and a rudimentary innkeeper living on the edge of the world, had all grown accustomed to our comforting presence. A great wind had blown up that afternoon, not an unusual event, but one with gusts so fierce we had to shut down our small boat traffic to and from the shore, wave off the submarine we had planned on repairing, and resign ourselves to riding out the blow. We had just checked that everything topside was properly battened down when we received a call from the mainland. A drunk had wandered out into the wind and snow. When the search dogs found his body, he was still breathing, but his internal temperature was in the low eighties. The local doctor believed the man had less than an hour to live without sophisticated medical care. The *McKee* had the only medical facilities within a thousand miles. A large commercial fishery ship in the harbor had volunteered their helo if our doctors would try to save him!

There was a roaring wind, large waves, and swirling sea spray as far as the eye could see across Cold Bay. If the commanding officer hadn't forced practicing this evolution to the point of boredom, do you think we would have risked the twenty men and women in our ship's landing crew as well as the three heroes in the helicopter? All for one drunk?

Even then it was an exciting several minutes!

After the victim recovered, we found out that he didn't imbibe. The "drunk" was actually a world traveler with an undiagnosed diabetic condition who was suffering from insulin deprivation. He had been the veritable innocent lamb—his diabetic reaction triggered by the severe cold—disoriented, wandering out into the weather looking for help.

Leadership involves preparing long, long before any need is evident. Preparation is the way a dangerous challenge metamorphoses into a satisfying memory.

6 ★ LOOKING DOWN

I CAN'T WATCH THE GAMBLING SCENE in the 1942 film *Casablanca* where Captain Louis Renault is "shocked, shocked" about gambling going on without being transported back in time. Not to the heat of Morocco, but to when I was young and eager and my commanding officer seemed like a pathological liar.

The man engaged in all sorts of behavior inimical to the organization's stated ethics, but since he didn't directly involve me or my family, I foolishly tried to ignore him and work on. His personal behavior only got more erratic with time. Among his transgressions, he was committing adultery in an organization that valued honor and integrity. He also was lying about nearly everything. His acts were so bare-faced, it seemed obvious that his bosses must know about and condone his behavior. Our ship quickly became progressively an ever worse place to work as good people voted with their feet. Those who had a choice left the Navy. Those constrained by a contract worked to get themselves transferred. In all this turmoil, I was eventually moved up to be his executive officer.

Many years later, long after that man had retired, I got up the gumption to ask the now snowy-white-haired man who had been his boss why he permitted the commanding officer to keep his job. The white-haired man actually was shocked. It wasn't the feigned reaction of *Casablanca*'s character Captain Renault. This real captain truly had no idea what I was talking about. By this time, it had been nearly two decades since the events. I had even published a book about the experience. I spoke heatedly for ten or fifteen minutes.

This ex-boss grew more dismayed with each minute, but he graciously waited until I was through. He swore to me that he had never been aware of the commander's lying and debauchery. He recalled that the man had successfully met all the established metrics. I looked in his eyes and he appeared honestly flustered, as if he were hearing new information for the first time.

Which returned the button to me. Why hadn't I gone to my commander's boss earlier? I had the credibility of being the number two. I knew better than anyone that the commander's behavior was out of bounds. I had less to lose than others. There were no golden handcuffs or family needs keeping me in that job. I could easily have shifted careers into a more lucrative field. I hadn't reported his behavior simply because I was positive all his seniors knew. When I failed to act I stole their opportunity to be leaders.

And consequently the commander continued to harm or destroy Navy individuals for another decade.

All because I thought (hoped) that his evaluators could accurately "see" down.

No one can. You may actually think you are pretty good at judging subordinates. You may think that because your underlings are always looking up at you like sunflowers, trying to perennially show you a smiling face, that you can see beyond those visages. You can't.

You may feel like the second coming of Santa, you know, the jolly overweight soul who can discern those who are good from the ones who deserve coal in their stockings, the supervisor who whisks in, takes a few hours to walk around, and announces they know all they need to know about the state of morale and condition of the organization. I have met people who say they can do just that.

They are full of it.

I have never met anyone who can fully and accurately evaluate even his or her first-level subordinates. In fact, while walk-arounds may be useful for morale purposes, the most successful manager I ever knew was Admiral Rickover, and he insisted that his supervisors periodically stand in one spot for a minimum of two hours just to learn what was happening within a few feet of themselves!

Personal evaluations are terribly difficult to get right, especially when the individual has a personality flaw he has successfully hidden for a long time. The really bad ones have been stinking their whole lives! When you meet them, it will be like meeting the murderer in a mystery novel, but most often no one will give you any clues! You aren't responsible for selecting the next Apostles; you are only looking for those men and women who will most rapidly advance the goals of the organization. But every now and then you need to feel responsible for identifying and eliminating the subversive who is carrying seeds of institutional destruction: alcoholism, abuse, pathological lying, etc.

Good luck. Reviewing subordinates is as difficult as a prospector looking out across desert sands. The shimmering heat often ensures that the miner can observe only that which exists somewhere else! Flawed people, especially the smart ones, are hard to identify. The awry individual has been hiding his or her tracks for a lo-o-o-ong time. I don't have a solution. But you need to be cautioned. This is much, much harder than you think or others believe.

(For more on this same subject, see "Red Flags and Warnings" in part 2.)

7 ★ HARD BODIES OR LEADERS?

THE VORACIOUS DESIRE FOR NEW FACES and new stories seems to guarantee that each of us will, in artist Andy Warhol's famous words, "be world-famous for fifteen minutes." But there is no guarantee it will be the best quarter-hour you ever have! No one implied you were going to get any advance warning. Or that your fifteen minutes on the screen will be positive. Which means, for those of us who would grasp for the leadership role, we must do our very best all the time—every minute—for as long as we wish to serve in that role.

I once was working with the people in the submarine rescue business when they got their opportunity. Unfortunately, some of them were having an off day when their call came for "lights, camera, action."

A submarine is susceptible to being accidentally run over, especially in the fog that clings to the edges of harbors. This vulnerability is enhanced by the low profile of the submarine, as well as its poor maneuverability on the surface. To counter these problems, the submarine is divided into several watertight compartments. Thus if a submarine is in a collision and the water is relatively shallow, the crew in the unbroached compartments will probably survive the initial unplanned voyage to the bottom. Since the crewmembers often have only the air in their undamaged section to breathe, the long-term survival of the men and women in those compartments will be largely dependent on how long it takes rescuers to arrive. Given that there is always time lost before it is realized a submarine is in trouble and that the position of the wreckage on the bottom may be in doubt, the reaction time of the rescue crew is critical.

American submarines represent the United States in every one of the seven seas. Worldwide submarine rescue is thus an American imperative. The high expense of a rescue system is considered part and parcel of the cost of having a submarine force. The rescue equipment to recover the crew is heavy and bulky, but also refined. A well-rehearsed team is essential. Air-deployable assets prepared in advance are also necessary. Because few nations can afford the cost of all this infrastructure, others usually content themselves with designing their submarines to be compatible with "big brother's" rescue equipment.

On the U.S. side, once you have acquired the equipment and established and trained a team to save your own submarines, you have much more capability than you need. It's like owning a posthole digger. Without one, digging a hole is really hard, but with one you can dig two holes nearly as easily as one. Since we have the capability, we could probably rescue a downed submarine about every other month. Historically, however, there is less than one survivable submarine casualty a decade. Nevertheless, to be ready for the once-in-a-lifetime (certainly for the rescue people who must be in peak physical condition) event, managers need to find related work to keep the team constantly sharp. The individuals assigned to this rescue mission are a special sort, primarily underwater divers and doctors selected for their willingness to work under stressful conditions. These men and women routinely need to maintain extraordinary physical conditioning and work at tasks that sharpen their ability to focus in the underwater environment. Consequently, in their "off-time" they work in deep-diving underwater research—taking scientists down to explore what happens in the vicinity of volcanic vents on the floor of the ocean, recovering expensive or irreplaceable items that have ended up on the bottom of the sea, and laying underwater cables for government agencies—demanding tasks intended to mimic actions they might take in a recovery.

This organization was one of the groups that reported to me. I got to see it in action and I even journeyed several thousand feet deep with them. One of the key rescue components they used was a battery-powered minisubmarine designed to mate with any possible downed submarine on the bottom of the ocean. It would then shuttle survivors back to another submarine or to a surface ship. If you ever saw the film *The Hunt for Red October* you watched the actors (and several regular Navy men recruited especially for the film) being so transported between the Soviet submarine *Red October* and the equally imaginary U.S. submarine *Dallas*.

But while many aspects of this group were interesting, the point of this case study involves leadership, not hard bodies or interesting hardware.

One night a diesel submarine belonging to one of our South American allies was accidentally run over by a surface ship and sunk. Our

group in San Diego responsible for submarine rescues received noti-
fication of this accident, as did I. It was every submariner's worst fear
and the very reason for the existence of our rescue unit!

By the time we learned of the accident, the South American submarine had already been down four hours. The location was a ten-hour
flight away. Loading the minisub and its gear would take three to five
hours, even if the Air Force managed to immediately produce the right
transport aircraft. Few diesel submarines have more than twenty-four
hours of available oxygen in any compartment. This meant we were
already working with razor-thin margins. Time was of the essence.

It was 3 a.m. when I heard about the casualty. I quickly dressed and
went down the hill from my home to watch a well-oiled machine operate.

When I arrived in the minisub hangar, neither the boss nor his
number two were yet there. I instead encountered a loud ongoing
argument among the three dozen people who had been called in from
their beds.

"It's too far away. We could never get there in time."

"I'm not sure we have an agreement on file with that country that
requires us to provide them rescue services. I can't locate it. I'm surprised Washington notified us."

"If we do anything, it will cost money. Who is going to pay for it?"

"We have a tough schedule to maintain. I was supposed to take Dr.
Steele out to view the underwater volcanic vents later today."

"From the charts, looks like they're in pretty shallow water. They
can probably get out on their own."

"Should we wait for more information?"

I may have listened for thirty seconds before taking charge and telling everyone we were going to respond and no one was to waste any
more time in discussion. Furthermore, they were going to break all
previous records getting the equipment over to North Island where it
could be loaded into an aircraft and launched. I got everyone moving.
Thirty minutes later their boss showed up and began organizing everything in the right direction. I stayed several hours until I was sure the
group had regained its mojo.

It was astounding to me that anyone in the team was even contem-
plating skipping a once-in-a-lifetime opportunity. Every person in the
team needed to be at their peak physical capability to even be considered for membership, so no one should have even anticipated being

personally around five to ten years later if and when another event might occur. Somehow they had all become invested in their routine schedule of "make work" and had completely lost any vision of the larger mission.

Our rig, complete with trained divers and doctors, was circling to land in the South American country when the last of the trapped submariners made their own escape. As I recall, only one of the submarine sailors died, and he did so in a heroic action that saved some of his injured shipmates.

By the time our team returned, the group had digested what had nearly not happened that evening and had discovered a renewed appreciation of their purpose. Some of the members had also experienced an interesting trip to an exotic city they would otherwise never have seen. There hadn't been any press coverage of the flight and visit. The country with the problem had handled it on their own, and, given their success, the political party in power was not particularly interested in advertising any relationships with their North American "big brother." Wonder what they would have done if we had delayed an hour or two, until we received clearance from Washington, or started our rescue preparations only after the submarine's own rescue attempts had failed and some or all of the men were dead?

We uncovered some problems in the way the unit was organized and trained. Those were fixed. We did completely destroy the rescue organization's schedule. No planned event was completed on time for at least a couple of weeks. Too bad.

There are few organizations of hard bodies trained to save lives under extreme conditions. One would think these groups would be veritable crucibles of leadership. But any team can become focused on the debris of day-to-day interactions and fail to recognize once-in-a-lifetime or life-and-death opportunities when they arise.

This was not a good Andy Warhol moment.

Who stops people from standing around while men are dying? Not the managers who write schedules. Not the hard bodies or people who maintain hardware. Managers prepare for and make routine events occur. Leaders make things happen.

Leaders. Leaders. Leaders.

8 ★ WAR GAMES

THE "WAR GAME" IS A TOOL THAT CAN be used to lift people out of the rut of their daily thinking. A "game" may get as complicated as the funds (and participant patience) available and can range from the simplest paper exercise (Team Blue does this for move one, the umpires describe the consequences, Team Orange decides to do Y for move two, etc.) to the electronic equivalent of opposing teams pushing wooden ships on a papier-mâché ocean. War gaming is often invaluable in ensuring that complex situations are understood.

The Naval War College in Newport, Rhode Island, was an early hotbed of war gaming. Concepts were practiced in those salt-encrusted granite buildings long before the science gained any footing within the military and several decades before it became popular with the public. There are always shortcomings in the process, but when done well, it prods participants, even staid admirals, to expand their horizons. If individuals don't consider new ideas, they at least are forced to consider the big picture. In a letter to the president of the Naval War College shortly after World War II about the prewar war games, Fleet Adm. Chester Nimitz, Commander in Chief U.S. Pacific Fleet and Pacific Ocean Areas, noted that because of their war games, during the actual conflict only the Japanese kamikaze aircraft had surprised him.

This is a case study about just such a war game. In the normal course of events, our world is a large, complicated, and changing place. Our armed forces are constantly thinking about the different roles they might be expected to perform. As circumstances and technology change, and manpower permits, components continually update their local plans. Some of these plans, such as a reaction to an attack on South Korea, are very specific. They are constantly updated as Army and Marine Corps units, Air Force wings, Navy ships and aircraft, and Coast Guard cutters rotate on assignment to the Western Pacific theater. The OpPlan for Korea is very detailed, with lots of annexes and each land, air, and naval component as well as allies having a role, minute by minute, from time GO to the conclusion of hostilities.

In the Pacific, along with the grand plan against the Soviets, at one time the Korean Plan was one of our most complicated efforts. It was so because it involved all our allies, as well as all five branches of the U.S. military. As a result, a week was set aside every other year to war-game the plan to ensure everyone understood their roles. All the military staffs spent several months preplanning the play, but the focus of this game was several days in which the actual decision makers were involved. Different years focused on different aspects of the engagement. In the game this vignette discusses, the admirals, generals, and other senior commanders were personally brought to Seoul, Korea, for three days and presented with the "problem" as it had been advanced to that point by their staffs (without the commander's input) and asked for their initial input. At this point, acceleration "magic" was applied by the controllers to quickly advance time in order to force the entire chain to react with appropriate communication delays and breakdowns, etc., to proceed to a second decision point for the senior commanders.

The value of a war game of this sort depends on the depth of the months of preparation—particularly how much thought has gone into including black swan events and their real possibility—and how well the controllers have duplicated and included the coordination, logistical, tactical, and communication difficulties of real life. Because the planners have been living with their game for several months and the staffs being "gamed" are fresh out of the field, where they have been focused on real-world events and inevitably not prepared nearly as well as the game planners, often the junior game controllers appear (to the operating staffs) to be a little snarky about clues the players miss or aspects the players could have done better.

Even if the game controller comments have real merit, the players have often been doing real-world work day and night at sea with little sleep, and just one arched eyebrow by a shore-based controller may well ensure that a valid comment will never be well received.

That week we had one controller who spent more than a few hours not so subtly letting everyone on my staff know that he personally was not terribly fond of submariners. After the final whistle blew on this particular game, we had killed nine North Korean submarines with no losses of our own and had received many accolades (my staff and I were in charge of the U.S. submarines in the Western Pacific).

Nevertheless, the controller had just walked out of our space with an over-the-shoulder comment that "if the game had only run another half-hour, one of your precious boats would be sitting on the bottom!" My operations officer had promptly kicked the door shut while loudly wishing he had been able to kick the snark's butt and directed the staff to pack our personal copies of the OpPlans, charts, computers, and files in the trunks for the flight home.

I had been awake for most of the five days of the exercise, so I tried to sleep on the C-130 Hercules flight back to Yokosuka, Japan, but I couldn't. It wasn't the noise or the webbed seats. When we landed, instead of heading off to my see my family, I asked one of my best lieutenants, Judy Cronin, to accompany me back to headquarters. We soon located a relatively empty fifteen-by-twenty-foot room in which it would be possible to construct a waist-high table.

I knew the controller hadn't been talking about an enemy submarine. No enemy submarine could hope to defeat a U.S. one. So it must have been a stray mine. There was no way I could have mistakenly ordered one of our submarines into a minefield, was there? If I had, that was a serious mistake. We had been working from real documents. We might execute that particular war plan any day. I needed Judy to check.

There is a finite amount of sea space around Korea. For the convenience of seagoing nations (e.g., to keep ships from running into each other in peacetime or shooting each other in wartime), that water is divided. Some is kept sacrosanct for the passage of commercial vessels and some is divided into sea lanes for war ships. Then there are completely restricted areas. The sea lanes are for ships and submarines to approach Korea during wartime. The restricted areas are those areas that can be mined so surface ships need not worry about Korean submarines popping out and shooting them at night. The theory was that no one would attack from a mined area because no ship or submarine would survive a minefield transit.

This was all great conceptually, but I knew from the confident look the snark had thrown over his shoulder that the man knew something I didn't. I had recently come from Washington, DC. I understood overlapping jurisdictions. While driving around our country's fair capital, there were more than twenty law enforcement organizations in the District of Columbia authorized to make an arrest! What about in the waters off Korea? I knew which of America's enemies might lay mines off Korea, and we attentively monitored those evildoers. But how many friendly organizations were authorized to lay mines in the waters off Korea? Who was watching them?

Lieutenant Cronin was going to find out.

Submarines lay precisely located minefields, and they can do so in enemy-controlled waters, but they insert patterns very slowly. There were only two areas appropriate for submarine-laid minefields. I asked Judy to lay out the charts of the waters around Korea and then attach see-through tissue paper overlaid with the boundaries for the potential submarine minefields shown in blue. Surface ships can also lay mines. They lay them faster than submarines and with the same accuracy, but for obvious reasons they don't do this in contested waters near land or where the enemy has control of the air. I tasked Judy to lay out the areas authorized for surface ship mining on a different tissue paper, with their area hatched in brown.

Navy airplanes also lay mines. They lay them a few at a time in critical spots from low altitudes. Tactical airplanes can fly in low and fast and place mines into contested areas. The aircraft may be avoiding flak as they make their runs. Their accuracy may vary depending on the pilot's training and personal verve. I wanted these in orange.

Air Force bombers lay mines. A B-52 can dump a lot of mines. A B-52 can plant an entire field in one sortie. They do so from an altitude well above small arms fire. At the time they did it a little less accurately than anyone else. I wanted these in a different color on another sheet.

The Japanese were also tasked with laying mines. After all, this was a war with their neighbor. Okay, show those, they were using the same navigation equipment as their U.S. counterparts. Different training standards, new colors. Same for the Koreans, it was their country we were defending! They used different equipment. Another set of colors.

Judy worked three long weeks on her project. In the end she had seventeen different tissue-thin overlays of seventeen slightly different tints laid atop one large chart of the Sea of Japan. There probably would be some great way to do it today with a computer that would save all that paper, but Judy figured out a way to fold each sheet and the chart so it all opened up like an origami rose. She had determined that in all the pressure to lay mines to protect the ships, even without any navigation error or jitters from pilots who might be under fire, we

Adm. Jim Hogg, one of the great intellectuals of the Navy. Always maintained his poise and presence, even under the pressure of extraordinary events. *U.S. Navy*

were placing mines into every last one of the submarine sea lanes that led into Korea! The snark had only noticed one of the conflicts!

I found an appropriate briefcase and took her magnificent product to my boss. Vice Adm. Jimmy Hogg watched me make the precise unfolds and listened to my explanation. He slowly cleaned his glasses and looked over the complete layout and promptly sent me and my chart, with its seventeen colored overlays, on his personal airplane back to his boss in Hawaii. Adm. Ace Lyons asked me to spread my chart out on the big table in his Honolulu office, and he quietly watched as I unfolded, explained, unfolded, unfolded once again, smoothed out a crease, and talked. Ace didn't say a word until I finished. Then he directed that particular war plan be immediately rewritten and republished to eliminate all the conflicts.

Leaders can learn valuable lessons during war games. For a major game, a staff may have worked several months to fashion stressful challenges or unfamiliar situations intended to create an environment for the leadership to develop new concepts or appreciations. My experience was that most participants did not take full advantage of this opportunity to think and learn. They were too busy trying to look good to their peers and bosses. If you are busy making up excuses for every time you fall short, you may well miss the opportunity to improve.

If you are really alert, you might even have an original thought or two.

9 ★ EARLY MORNINGS AND LATE NIGHTS

LEADERSHIP IS A DIFFICULT ATTRIBUTE TO DEFINE. No matter that you may tell people you are a leader, are you really? Do you even believe you make a difference?

A good friend of mine was once leaving a job where he had command for four years. During that time the ship and her crew had done reasonably well in myriad challenges. In the process, the ship had become known as a "hot ship." The officer who would be taking over for my friend had held a special job in the Bureau of Naval Personnel. Because he could, "Brad" had pulled a few strings to get this particular command. He also had been able to select who would be his executive officer and engineer (the key two jobs on a nuclear submarine). I knew all the people involved and both the individuals he had selected. They were exceptional. Brad had clearly stacked the talent deck at the expense of all the other submarines in the Navy. In fact, there were specific guidelines against doing what he had done. We didn't have enough exceptional people in the submarine force to afford two such officers on only one ship, but Brad's supervisor had been lax. Brad was already on the fast track for admiral and knew it, and he planned to make his tour aboard his new ship the platform to cement his case.

One abnormal facet of the change of command was that the submarine was in overhaul, so Brad wouldn't have the opportunity to ride and observe the ship at sea before he took responsibility. That was unusual, but the powers that be had decided it was acceptable. Brad and the man he was relieving both had about twenty years of experience in the Navy. They had each served on three other submarines. During the turnover process, Brad had several days to poke into every corner and privately speak to the officers and crew to find out how the ship had been run.

Which led to the conversation I had later with my friend while playing pool at the Submarine Sanctuary in Yokosuka, Japan. My friend swore that they reached the point in the process that the only thing left was for Brad to sign the paperwork to assume responsibility for the reactor core and some nuclear sources. These were theoretically possible to misplace, but only theoretically.

This is the story Rob told me:

Brad surprised him by saying he wanted to talk. He brought his cup of coffee into the Commanding Officer's office and closed the door.

"Rob, I understand that you have made it a practice to personally go to control whenever the ship is proceeding to periscope depth."

"Yes."

"I understand from the officers of the deck that even if it is the middle of the night. Even when the situation on the surface is so benign that they have reported there are no close contacts." Rob swore that Brad looked at him inquisitively.

"No close contacts" meant that sonar believed there were no surface ship threats within several miles. And Rob replied, "Yes."

"And that when you give them permission to proceed up from 120 feet, that when they reach periscope depth and they say to the chief of the watch, 'Call the captain and tell him I am at periscope depth and have no visual contacts,' that each and every time they will hear your voice from someplace behind them in the dark of the control room, 'I have the word.'"

"Yes."

Brad looked directly in Rob's eyes and took a sip of his coffee. By now, Rob was more than interested. It looked like Brad was trying to make this coffee klatch a teachable moment for Rob. "Rob, I think you should have made these officers grow more on their own. You have taught them how to safely go up to periscope depth. I think you should have stayed in your stateroom. By coming to control you demonstrated you do not actually trust them to do the job you qualified them to do."

Rob looked him straight in the eyes. "Brad, going to periscope depth is the most dangerous evolution a submarine does. The reason submarines are so invulnerable is not because you and I are personally cool or Admiral Rickover is such a SOB, but because the acoustics change so dramatically in the top hundred feet of the oceans." Brad tossed his head in a way that made Rob think that rather than listening, he was considering whether or not he had time to get a haircut before the change of command ceremony.

Rob picked his pool cue back up and tried to line up a shot and then stopped. His hands were shaking. "I tried to make Brad understand how serious I was."

"The only reason more submarines aren't lost to collisions is because of the big-ocean-few-ships thumb rule. Our submarine will go to periscope depth a maximum of three or four times a day and every time it does, you, as captain, will have ten to sixteen years more experience than anyone on board, including the individual looking through the periscope! Every now and then it is possible sonar is going to be absolutely wrong and there will be a deep draft tanker coming directly at you and the tanker's huge bulk is hiding the noise from his screw. Sonar won't hear that tanker until your ship gets very shallow and then the sound will suddenly explode from all around you and a young officer may be confused or freeze. There are 130 other people on board this ship. If that happens some night, who do you think each officer of the deck's shipmates would prefer to have standing in the back of control where he can bring those years of experience to bear?"

Rob wondered if Brad was still thinking about his hair; it was a bit long around the ears. He was still thinking about his responsibility. He rephrased his last question to him, "Who do you think all of their parents would prefer to have in the back of the control room?"

Rob told me Brad had only shifted in his chair, drained his cup of coffee, and changed the subject.

It might have been only an interesting story told over the green felt of a pool table. But there was more, for the submarine force emphasizes personal responsibility and long command tours are integral to that concept. There is no being lucky for six to twelve months, checking the command box, and then going to an ashore job and saying that you are prepared to be promoted. In this particular case, three years later, while in the process of coming to periscope depth, Brad's submarine came up underneath a freighter. Brad subsequently had to drydock his submarine for repairs.

I had nearly forgotten the story and the name when Brad called me at home several years later. Brad informed me he was in the zone for selection to flag officer. He wanted to acquaint me with all the high honors his submarine had won while he was in command. He asked me to put in a good recommendation to my fellow flag officers who might be sitting on Brad's selection board. He didn't mention his collision, which Thucydides long ago correctly noted will ruin a sailor's whole day. He also didn't mention that asking me to attempt to influence the flag selection board was completely counter to proper Navy personnel practices.

I told Brad I had heard of him.

Brad never became a flag officer in the U.S. Navy.

Let me backtrack for just a moment. Rob had been absolutely correct! I have always thought that the question of whether or not to physically be in the control room while the submarine is going to periscope depth was the easiest question in submarining. Most large ships have drafts of less than fifty feet. A supertanker has a hull (draft) that goes down as much as ninety feet below the water. Submarines are going to prepare to come to periscope depth by doing a careful acoustic search at a depth where their sail is not going to be inadvertently hit by one of these deep-draft ships. The water between a submarine and the surface is affected by the sun, the wind, the waves, and sea life. It is a mess! You do not want to waste time getting from the initial safe depth to the point that you can visually see any problems. At the same time, on the way up, as different acoustic paths change, an experienced seaman may suddenly realize that danger is present; a ship headed directly at you has the smallest sonar signature, but it often changes as the sound bounces off the different layers in the ocean as the submarine becomes shallower. The man or woman on the periscope is worried about many things—and if it is an old periscope, about ignoring the water down the back of their necks—and may not be able to assimilate the various noise changes from the various sensors and what they might imply.

Since the act of going to periscope depth has been the process by which the United States has lost the most submarines in peacetime, if your son or daughter is on board a submarine, tomorrow morning at 2 a.m., would you like his or her life to be in the hands of a fully qualified twenty-four-year-old? A real superstar with lightning reflexes who had done at least a dozen similar processes in achieving that qualification? Or would you prefer that superstar be conducting the evolution while being closely overseen by an old salt who had previously performed this very evolution thousands of times in six different oceans?

I observed coming to periscope depth each time any ship of mine made the transition from deep to near-surface during the four years I was in command. Day and night. I did it when I was feeling good or when I might have a roaring headache. I considered it to be part of my contract with my crew.

As most of you may not occupy yourselves running submarines or going to periscope depth, reflect for a moment on your own leadership team. During normal working hours, you have your entire leadership and management team, if not involved, at least available. They thus are available to provide the "casual" leadership any organization needs. This includes such items as the constant gleaning of the tone of conversations (are people excessively worried about the planned move, or the new person in HR, or the new goals?)

In fact, many small teams either deliberately balance themselves or have become balanced as different people pick up responsibilities. Each team often has its strong and weaker points. As a group, they manage quite well. But who is checking the back shifts? And who is walking through the off-sites? And what are the business hours in which you actually perform well? Not the front office business hours, but the working hours of the subgroups that have to set up and operate to make the organization work? How does the leadership team work with these groups?

I never figured out some way to exercise leadership with "records and reports." When I was in port or at a job that didn't involve a ship, the only way I knew to approach the problem was to walk around the facility late at night or early in the morning and talk to people about what they were doing. Often it was enough to do a walk-through right before I left at night. Sometimes after I had gone to an event in the evening I would come back to the job site before I went home. Infrequently I set an alarm and came in around 2 or 3 a.m., to show interest to whoever was working on whatever. Sometimes I just came in a bit early two or three days a week. Each time I did so I learned something I didn't know about the business—or established another informal bond with someone—and heard how an individual or a group believed we should best operate his job, or how someone believed misfeasance was happening. I was their leader.

Late nights are conducive to good days.

10 ★ DAYDREAMING

LEADERS PREPARE THEMSELVES. And they prepare themselves for the expected challenge. Is your ultimate goal a particular distance race? Achieving a number of pull-ups? Or will it involve resolve? If you routinely spend an hour a day working on your body's core strength, how many minutes should you spend preparing your mind for leadership challenges?

Many of us worry that success is a personality contest. We fear that the pleasant person chosen to lead the third grade Pledge of Allegiance will still be front and center when we are in our thirties or our forties. We agonize over whether our late night and early morning work will be for naught. We worry that our uniqueness will never be valued. But how much do you really lust to be a leader?

It is more than three thousand miles as the crow flies between the colored lights of Hong Kong to the cold tides that lap against the Russian submarine base of Petropavlovsk. "Petro" is a large, secluded port tucked into a crack in the Vostochny mountain chain. There, protected from prying eyes, is where the Russians repair and train their Pacific fleet of ballistic missile submarines.

Should an American submarine wish to proceed from the exceptional liberty in Hong Kong to "work" in the Russian operating areas off Petro, it has to take a more circuitous route, since there are reefs, rocks, and minefields along the "crow's route." It thus requires a week or more to make this particular voyage, and while our theoretical submarine would be on its hypothetical trip, even with the constant training and onboard "fixing" that is a staple of submarine life, there is also ample time for the crew to become bored, especially during those long hours after midnight, the time that all navies have historically called the "mid-watch."

These miserable hours were those when the majority of the crew was asleep and only a few of us were charged with remaining awake while the submarine literally rolled onward down the navigator's charted track. This was through an ocean area frequently swept by storms. In these waters large surface waves sometimes seize a round-bottomed submarine and mercilessly push it rolling down to depths of several hundred feet. During these long hours most of the transiting crew quietly hold on to stanchions to keep from being thrown about and watch gauges and machinery while gossiping to keep themselves alert, talking sports, lying about what they did in Hong Kong, making plans for a later port visit to Thailand.

I didn't participate in the conversation. Never. I used mid-watches for thinking.

The submarine force has the deserved reputation of "doing things by the book." It requires two people to perform even the simplest evolution. There is one person actually moving the valves, turning the knobs or pushing the buttons while someone else checks and reads the next step from the approved procedure. If something is so unusual as to not have an existing procedure, then one is developed and approved before the evolution is commenced.

But there are exceptions.

There are a dozen or so potentially dangerous casualties in which the initial response is time-critical. In these limited cases, there are specific immediate actions to be carried out without resort to any manual, book, or "cheat sheet." When I wasn't busy on the mid-watches, I was testing myself on these "dirty dozen."

I also used the time to force myself to mentally explore what might happen further down each of these dirty dozen roads. What would I do after the immediate action was completed? The manuals only dealt with the early actions. Okay, I had now memorized what initially to do and the technical manuals often discussed some of the next steps. But what might unfold after that? Or if the problem got worse?

How bad might it get?

What would I do?

When would I lose control of the situation?

When would it no longer matter what I might desire to do?

For me, these "daydreams" were more fruitful than discussing the most recent sports scores the submarine had received over the wire the previous night. I wanted to think these professional situations through in advance. Like a golfer approaching an unfamiliar green, I needed to play each shot and, when I did not like the result, reset and play another approach until I had exhausted all the possible places a golf ball might roll. I needed to know when only courage would prevent me from going out of bounds. As I replayed these situations again and again in my mind, I decided I had uncovered some specific insights:

- You have a limited period of time to affect a problem,
- Dawdlers become swamped by events, and
- Deciding not to act is itself a decision.

Soon I was placed in a situation in which I could apply what I had learned.

The United States had decided to carry nuclear weapons on board submarines. Immediately the powers that be began worrying about what the Russians might learn if a submarine went down and the Russians recovered an intact nuclear weapon. While scientists across America leapt to their slide rules (this was a while ago) to figure out a sophisticated technical solution, the submarine force adopted an interim approach. One might refer to it as a brute force method. A wooden case of TNT was procured for each nuke and the top of the case pried off. Twelve-inch fuses were then attached to each stick of dynamite and the box was then slid under the nuclear-tipped anti-submarine rockets and wedged into place. If, against all odds, the submarine was pinned down by the Soviets and the crew considered abandoning ship, we were to light one of the fuses. This was easy. Since nearly everyone in the crew at the time smoked and all of us carried one of those steel-case Zippo lighters, someone could just toss a lighter into the box. Problem solved! The open boxes of TNT seemed like a foolproof plan to protect this advanced U.S. nuclear technology.

Nobody in our ship had any desire for an early visit to Kingdom Come, so we didn't permit smoking in the torpedo room within ten feet of the two open cases of the dynamite under the two torpedo skids that held the nuclear weapons. Unfortunately, as Robert Burns might say, "The best laid plans of mice and men gang aft agley," and early one morning I was awakened by chilling words over the 1MC (a broadcasting system that blares all over the submarine): "fire in the torpedo room."

I rolled out of my bunk and headed forward toward the torpedo room. On my way I noticed all the fourteen other officers on board were headed aft toward the control room. They were apparently going to manage the situation from there. I remember thinking they were making an interesting choice. There was only one passage in the ship to and from the torpedo room. By procedure, in about two seconds, that passage was to be closed and locked, not to be reopened until the casualty was solved. I was the junior, least experienced officer on board. After the dogs in the watertight door spun shut, I would be the only officer at the fire site. If I succeeded in putting out the fire, we would all live. If I did not, everyone would die.

If a nuclear weapon went off, everyone on board would live only some fraction of a second longer than I. I heard the clang of the torpedo room watertight door shutting behind me. Who in their right mind would leave me alone in here?

The flames were coming from the bilge. Some waste oil had caught fire, probably from a poorly extinguished cigarette butt. Of the ship's crew of 130, there were now 6 of us in the torpedo room. As soon as I looked at the TNT, I instantly knew our most immediate concern! During one of my interminable mid-watches I had researched dynamite. I knew the colorless drops beginning to collect on the bottom of one of the boxes were nitroglycerin! The heat from the bilge flames was causing the dynamite to begin a sublimation process. The relatively stable dynamite was decomposing into nitroglycerin before our very eyes! Once it is decoupled from the inert binder of the sticks, nitro is unstable. By itself it is susceptible to shock and might explode at anytime. We unwound a fire hose. The drops on the bottom of the boxes were getting bigger. Now they were about to drop! Two of us shifted the fire hose to the fog mode and aimed it into the bilge directly below the boxes of dynamite to try to cushion the drops while the others broke out dry chemicals for the flames dancing in the bilge.

We watched helplessly as a couple of the nitro drops hit the steel bilge and slid down. We waited for the flash. Thankfully the hull of the ship was curved where the drops landed. Maybe that cushioned their landing? A little more fog underneath the boxes. I was a lot more worried about the nitro than the fire! More water on the dynamite box to cool it. The fuses were already wet. Were there fewer drops? More chemicals on the fire in the bilge. Were the oil flames any lower? Damn the smoke!

Control wanted to know the status. There were asking over the 1MC because we weren't providing enough information over the sound-powered phones. All of us in the torpedo room were busy holding our breath.

The flame popped out.

A large drop formed on the side of the starboard box and joined together with several others on the forward corner. It was larger than any we had previously seen. We directed the fog down into the bilge below that box again. The water mist rose. Was it cushioning the drop? Who knew? We held our breath. The drop hung, quivered and fell . . . no explosion.

The smoke was now just hanging in the air about chest level, but it had stopped getting thicker. I stepped closer and looked carefully at the dynamite. No more drops were forming on the outside of the box. We would have to be careful no one "helpfully" used a putty knife on the runny residue the nitro runs had left. It was time to fill in all those supervisors eighty feet away, crowded into the control room. On my mid-watches, it had not gone as well. My concern one night was what had led me to look up all the characteristics of TNT. And on board a submarine, all knowledge is valuable, for you either slay each dragon that rears its ugly head or the dragon roasts you.

How much of leadership is mental preparation? I can't parse which portions are the most important. But I do wonder how anyone can ever hope to lead if they don't work at mentally preparing themselves.

11 ★ REFOCUSING

WHEN PROBLEMS ARE REALLY DIFFICULT, they often resist solution by normal leadership techniques. In these cases, find something new. And if the first, second, or third effort doesn't work, the real leader never gives up. She or he keeps working the problem. Keep turning the situation over in your mind while looking for new opportunities.

Adm. Bud Zumwalt was the Navy's Chief of Naval Operations during a period in which the Navy had a list of "number one problems" longer than a snake's belly: ships worn out from the high operating tempo of the Vietnam War, widespread racism, the internal stress involved in converting the submarine force from diesel to nuclear, and all the decisions involved in fighting the Vietnam War (there was no Joint Staff at the time). The CNO told me several times during 1972 (to orient the reader, this was the year after Daniel Ellsberg had leaked the Pentagon Papers) that the Vietnam War was lost and his personal focus was on how to get a racist and misogynist Navy safely into the future. National birth rates were telling us that our future sailors would be primarily black, brown, and female. How was he to guide the Navy from the present to the future?

I believe his efforts during the mid-1970s were Admiral Zumwalt's most impressive accomplishments. I am going to break my discussion of what I took away from his teaching into several case studies. This one deals with the fact that leadership is hard. Hewing to a line skewed from the norm does not get easier over time. Staying the course is made easier if there is at least one soul who is your personal seraph. As is true for so many of us, for Bud Zumwalt it was his spouse.

Zumwalt believed the secret to getting a strong Navy of the future was to immediately begin solving institutional racism and harassment problems. The situation was wrong. He wasn't going to delay or accept excuses. Consequently, the admiral invented different measures to directly and indirectly work that issue. He wasn't aided a great deal by his staff. Most of us were white males.

Adm. Elmo Zumwalt. He could see clearly when others stumbled. He prepared the Navy for a world where women as well as black and brown people would be manning our defense ramparts. *Naval History & Heritage Command*

A lack of personal experience at the leadership level will nearly always exist when the need for change is advanced. The past history of racism in the Navy had made wide-scale recruitment, selection, and advancement of black, Latino/Latina, and female officers difficult. And there will also be hiccups. In this case, one of the black males selected to lead Admiral Zumwalt's antiracism efforts was a charming, seducing, womanizing blowhard. And of course, as I have discussed earlier, the admiral couldn't see it and thought the blowhard was terrific. The flawed man's personality cast sand in the gears of the admiral's racial program. As a leader, you need to realize that some of the people you choose as followers will prove to be weak reeds and will betray you.

To return to the staff's "white problem," while the other officers on his personal staff and I were doing our best to follow Admiral Zumwalt's guidance, each night when we went home, it was to our all-white or nearly all-white communities. And sometimes, if I were to be honest, I may have thought to myself, the Navy is fighting the Vietnam War, which may and may not be winnable, but President Nixon won't back away and people are still getting killed so I am working each day to support that war. And I am also concurrently working long hours six or seven days a week doing everything I can do to win the Cold War, a conflict that could result in the destruction of America. And now I need to take extra time to fix race relations, a subject that neither President Nixon nor the 1972 Congress cares anything about? And neither do any of the other services! Why is only the Navy trying to fix a national problem? I know I would have dropped my own efforts on race relations like a hot rock if the CNO had even momentarily relaxed his personal pressure.

Fortunately, Admiral Zumwalt had married a special person. His spouse was the late Mouza Zumwalt, or Mouza Coutelais-du-Roche Zumwalt to be more precise. She was the daughter of a French man and Russian woman. And my spouse, Linda, of all-English ancestry, had become friends with Mouza Coutelais-du-Roche Zumwalt. Since my sister was living with us and could occasionally look after our children, Mouza and Linda had a practice of spending Wednesday afternoons together. I should have been happy. A young officer's spouse had become friends with the CNO's wife. Must be good. Right?

Wrong.

In the early 1970s, even in northern Virginia, many public and semipublic facilities were effectively still segregated. This was true even in the places of worship, where black members were shunted to the back rows of the church or up to the balcony. Mouza had heard of this and was determined to do her own personal sit-ins. She and Bud lived in the District of Columbia at Thirty-Fourth Street off Massachusetts

Avenue at the Naval Observatory grounds. They were the last Navy couple to live in what is now the vice president's house. We lived in Virginia just over the Key Bridge. Every Wednesday, Mouza would collect Linda and the two of them would attend services in a different Virginia church. Once inside, they would sit with the black parishioners.

Each Wednesday evening, I asked the same question. "Was she crying?"

Linda knew I was inquiring about Mouza's condition when the two of them had left the church services. Her answer was usually "Yes."

I usually groaned in reply. Damn! The admiral could not bear to see Mouza cry. I can view this today with a great deal more equilibrium than I did then. By the next morning I knew our boss's fertile mind would have constructed some new way to hurry/push/accelerate the betterment of race relations in the Navy. Of course, he already had a program in place, and new actions were often disruptive to the previous plans. But on this subject, he often seemed more emotional than rational. And he was probably right. If he hadn't worked on race and sexual relations each and every day, the Navy would have easily slid backward on this issue.

I do know that each Wednesday I went to bed dreading what the next day would bring. That woman was keeping him too focused!

A leader needs a system to periodically recenter herself or himself on their goals. Formal systems will work. Personalized arrangements can be even more effective. Zumwalt's informal system was his beautiful spouse. She reminded him daily how much he despised racism. What is going to remind you of your core beliefs?

PART 2

Perennial Problems a Leader Will Encounter

12 ★ COLD BAY WOMEN

THE POPULATIONS OF OUR TWO peer economic competitors, China and India, are both just over 1.3 billion people. The United States is a quarter of that size. Decades of data indicate that geniuses as well as innovation tend to spring up from large groups. It seems obvious, even if we wish to ignore principles of fairness and equality, that if the United States desires to compete effectively within the world economically—and militarily—we must empower our women.

In the Navy, Adm. Bud Zumwalt first established the policy of employing women on board Navy ships in 1972. The first woman graduated from the Naval Academy in May 1980. While these changes received positive press at the time, there was uneven acceptance within the Navy, and a decade later in 1991, a backlash occurred in the naval aviation community that became widely known as the Tailhook scandal. Sexual equality has proven a difficult goal. The #MeToo cycle of 2018 is another public indicator of this problem. What will it take to actually reach success?

Humans tenaciously resist change. Modifying existing norms requires more than good intentions, a directive, and a rousing speech or two. That behavior should not surprise anyone. We use shared memories and tribal instincts to guide us through uncertainty. That is the good aspect of culture.

But what happens when the military wants to change long before local communities are willing to stop being racist and sexist? The military's youth come from those same communities. That is the challenge. The shared values of thousands of communities and churches don't fully support that switch. But we need a strong military working together to challenge America's enemies. Few American communities are focused on how America competes with China and India. Most are instead thinking about RVs, the next parent-teacher meeting, and next Friday night's football game. Community leaders may not focus on how racism and sexism weaken America.

Which is why the military has needed to lead in changing America on these issues. And the key is for the military leader to be confident. You can't doubt your goal. You will also have to take some personal risks. As Prof. John A. Shedd put it in his 1928 book *Salt from My Attic,* "A ship in harbor is safe—but that is not what ships are built for." Nor are leaders.

When Zumwalt announced he was allowing women to go to sea, there was an immediate uproar—as was to be expected. The Navy had delayed the move on women for two hundred years. Even the Secretary of the Navy, who had not been previously informed, immediately decried Admiral Zumwalt's words. The senior Navy leadership faced the usual problems from "culture fanatics" (e.g., the Old Guard) who would battle the very hint of change, particularly the individuals no longer involved day-to-day with the Navy. Some progress was made on sexism while he was CNO, but Zumwalt was much more focused on the race issue, which was the wolf nearest his sled (and President Nixon told him he could work on racism but to leave the women's issues alone). After Zumwalt retired, women were still being recruited but little effort was made to address the underlying cultural issues the Navy had with women.

Fifteen years after Admiral Zumwalt had been relieved as CNO, I took over an organization that made up about 10 percent of the afloat Navy. It was quickly apparent to me how little effort my predecessors had placed into making any gender equality policy succeed. Even if the concept were being superficially pressed by the very top of the Navy, it was obvious that the leadership at my command had been sitting on their butts. To begin with, wherever I looked, the male sailors did not respect the distaff ones.

I couldn't tell whether it was in reaction to the men's disdain, but it was also clear the women were reinforcing that stereotype by underperforming. Eleven percent of the unmarried women on board my twenty-odd surface ships were pregnant, which meant that according to current Navy policy the same 11 percent couldn't go to sea, and a disproportionately low number of women were qualified in the various shipboard teams (firefighting, damage control, etc.) critical to the at-sea survival of the ships. Both of these situations were unacceptable.

The key to any navy is to be at sea. But being at sea is often boring and uncomfortable. No matter how many Horatio Hornblower books you have read, except for the exhilaration of survival in a storm, or the adrenaline of a battle, even Horatio would rather be engaged in roguishness on land. Nevertheless, you don't learn to drive a truck by idling in the driveway, you don't learn to fly an airplane simply by spinning the engines on the ramp, and a sailor doesn't become a seaman in port. Just as it takes miles of inclement driving to make a long-haul trucker, it takes years at sea to develop a sailor.

Instead of being encouraged, these sailors had been invited to fail. They had been told, as soon as anyone realized they were pregnant, that because of the rare danger of an ectopic pregnancy (the fertilized egg attaches and begins to grow in one of the fallopian tubes), the women could no longer go to sea. I believed that our unmarried pregnancy rate of 11 percent was a direct consequence of poor leadership. I also believed the danger was medically unfounded and the policy was bred in the bias at senior Navy levels.

Most of my staff were appalled at the women's behavior. I wasn't. I knew that the average age of the women (and men) in the Navy was between nineteen and twenty years old. If the Navy was going to give eighteen- or nineteen-year-old women the choice between the unknown danger and discomfort of going to sea (something the average woman sailor had seen few, if any, other women do) or staying at home and having a baby (a task women had done for thousands of years), I suspected I knew what at least 10 percent of high-school-aged women would choose, no matter how destructive it might be to their future lives. At the same time, this behavior was affecting Navy readiness. If junior women got pregnant and couldn't go to sea, then there was no incentive to train child-bearing-age women for at-sea jobs, for the chances were demonstrably low that the young women would be on board when the ship sailed.

I had my doctors do some research. The medical staff soon found a fatal blood disease that only occurred in men that was roughly as rare as ectopic pregnancy. For my part, after several telephone calls I determined that no commercial oceanic steamship line screened its passengers for pregnancy nor cared if the women were. So if young rich women weren't dying from pregnancy complications at sea, and if the Navy didn't do a blood test before each ship got under way to prescreen men for a disease that had the same fatal results as ectopic pregnancy, weren't the current Navy rules factually and economically discriminatory?

The admiral who headed the Bureau of Navy Personnel was Vice Adm. Mike Boorda. He and I had both grown up on the lower end of the socioeconomic scale. I knew he wanted the women-in-the-Navy program to work. I called him and gave him my findings. I presented to him that we either should start giving a lot of unnecessary blood tests to all our male sailors or we should change our policy.

"I understand your logic. What exactly would you like, Dave?"

"I need the prohibition lifted on pregnant women going to sea."

"You know not everybody in our Navy or in Congress wants women to succeed." Mike paused. "I know that specifically some on the Surf-Pac staff and in Congress will say you will be endangering lives." There was a silence on the line but I sensed Mike wanted to help.

I did some quick mental calculations. I needed to give him a compromise. "Why don't you change the rules to permit pregnant women to go to sea as long as they are within twelve hours of transport to a hospital in the event of a medical emergency?"

"Let me talk to the Bureau of Medicine. I think they might go for six." I hadn't agreed the ship had to be within twelve hours of land. I was already thinking of a helo lift to a carrier, and a COD aircraft from the flattop to shore might well suffice to meet the time requirement. Mike was smart. I knew he had picked up on my omission.

I thanked him. "Admiral, I appreciate your consideration." Six hours might work in the Atlantic, where Mike had sailed most of his career, but it wouldn't work in the wide spaces of the Pacific. But once the absolute prohibition was gone, an interpretation would be possible, or even an "admiral-waiver." And once it was no longer policy that all pregnant women were to be given a pass to remain ashore, I was confident most of the young women would face up to their angst and go to sea rather than face the real alternative of becoming single mothers.

I have forgotten the final wording Mike published. But he got it out the next week. He was trying. It wasn't actually adequate for what we needed tactically, but it lifted the absolute prohibition. I could handle the personal risk of the "admiral-waiver" part.

Armed with this crack in the paper wall, we attacked the culture issue with new vigor. We found a senior woman doctor, a Navy captain, who was willing to provide birth control lectures. She divided up the ten thousand sailors in the command and began rotating them through discussions at about two hundred to five hundred twice a week. We installed condom and sponge dispensers in every ship's berthing areas, and the doctor's assistant kept them filled. I personally briefed the senior women about the need for them to take charge and set new expectations for the younger women.

And in the midst of this work (which probably would never have been sufficient) a great opportunity arose. At the time, we were in a Cold War with the Soviet Union and its Warsaw Pact allies. President Reagan's philosophy was to force Russia to surrender by continually raising the military stakes with technological challenges like the missile defense program, dubbed Star Wars. Reagan and his eventual successor, Vice President George H. W. Bush, had turned to challenging the Soviets in military areas in which we had a technological advantage. For years, we had been ratcheting up the pressure from our clearly superior submarine force. As a consequence, attack submarines in the Pacific were deploying against the Soviet Union for eleven to thirteen months at a time, with often only a few months for rest and retraining before the next mission.

Now Washington had decided to raise the stakes even higher with a dramatic exercise. In a few months all of our submarines on the West Coast would be sortied, along with the two San Diego submarine tenders, large ships that can do major submarine repairs. One of my tenders would head south to Bali in Indonesia, and the other would head north to Cold Bay, a port six hundred miles west of Anchorage. Cold Bay was essentially a wide spot in the road in the Aleutian island chain halfway between Alaska and Russia. Cold Bay was a particularly barren place, last visited by a Navy ship in 1945. It had two things to recommend it: the harbor and the airstrip. There was a large and deep harbor, once you were past the rocks that guarded the narrow entrance, and a full-length airstrip. The latter had been constructed as a defense against the Japanese during World War II and had been a stop on the air route to Murmansk. The airport was still operational. It and the fishing village were manned by eighty hardy souls, one or two of whom were annually lost to the large and powerful Kodiak bears that prowled around the area, normally feeding on seals and fish.

The point of this deployment was for Russian president Mikhail Gorbachev to suddenly discover over his borscht that he had lost all track of the U.S. nuclear submarine fleet! Was the United States increasing its defense posture? It was assumed that the Soviets would frantically search the world for the military assets they most feared and finally discover the submarines being quietly maintained in Bali and Cold Bay, bare-bones facilities to which we hadn't sent a ship in decades! The goal was to demonstrate to the Soviets that even if they were able to deliver a nuclear strike against the continental United States, our nuclear submarines could continue to fight on until every square inch of the Soviet Union was rubble.

This secret deployment was obviously serious business. The submarine admiral responsible for the Seattle area, where the ballistic missile submarines were homeported, would board the tender headed to Bali and I would place my flag on the repair ship headed for Cold Bay. The event was scheduled for late autumn, when the weather near Cold Bay promised to be iffy at best. We would encounter winds of at least a hundred knots and probably the tail end of a storm or two of at least gale force. According to satellite weather reports, snow was already on the ground in Cold Bay and what looked much like early skim ice was beginning to form around the edges of the harbor. If the Soviets located us quickly, we didn't know if they would send aircraft, ships, or Spetsnaz, so we would have to man armed outposts on the icy hills that surrounded the port. As soon as we briefed the crew, the air of danger throughout the ship became palpable.

I couldn't have asked for a better situation if I had been able to write the scenario: a wilderness, a challenge, and the possibility of an actual physical clash with the Soviets! By the time we returned to San Diego, I intended to have converted the tender's thirteen-hundred-person crew, 30 percent of whom were women, into believing they were one team.

The first day we were informed of this upcoming tasking I spent an hour with the ship's navigator and then informed Capt. Ralph Schlichter that I had looked at the track (the plot of where the ship intends to go relative to land) and air assets that would be available and had determined that all the ship's company (i.e., all the women, pregnant or not) were eligible to go to sea under the new BuPers guidelines. He looked at me questioningly. His suspicions were correct; my intentions were suspect. While his tender was helo-capable, staying within several hours of land would turn a ten-day trip into a three-week journey. Once out of sight of land, I fully intended to come left and take a more direct route.

I said, "If it makes you more comfortable, I recommend you write my statement down some place. I'll even be happy to sign it. But we are not discussing it any more and you have a lot of work to do to get ready for this deployment. You need to make sure everyone in the crew knows they are getting under way so they can plan accordingly and the teams can start training."

Ralph simply nodded and returned to the vast business of getting his ship prepared for the next several months. The flush of activity was perfect. While uncertainty is in the future, it is a mistake not to create a tidal wave of activity to sweep people along. There is no good reason to make it easy for an individual to have extra hours on his or her hands. All they will do is worry about the unknown. If forced to participate, most individuals will find courage on their own. On the other hand, if you don't give them a timely push, they will never have the opportunity to make the natural metamorphosis from gazelle to lion!

Some weeks later we were under way—firing every gun—another good idea Captain Schlichter came up with, ensuring that every man and every woman on board knew how the steel felt as it bucked in their hands. When you are on board a warship, off to a place where you will be the only law, there is nothing more comforting than going to sleep to the sound of gunfire from your own ship.

Once we arrived in the harbor at Cold Bay, we deployed the false ship radar targets we had welded together during the transit and anchored ourselves near two high cliffs. We thus maximized the Soviets' large-area identification problem and constrained the approach arcs for bombing aircraft. The tender immediately began planning how it would service the submarines that would come and go at night like deadly shadows while I looked for opportunities to cement the role of women in the crew. The first opening occurred as I listened to the ship's executive officer briefing the teams being sent out to secure the perimeter around the airport.

"We will rotate teams every two weeks. While you are out there you need to stay warm and alert. Even if the Soviets don't send Spetsnaz, remember that the bears here silently kill and eat one or two of the residents every year." The teams were about fifteen people in size, with three or four women in each one. Everyone was dressed in the orange Arctic gear the ship had obtained, although no one had yet donned the white snow parka. Most had the heavy jacket on the benches alongside them, along with their sixty-pound pack, since at least one hand was occupied holding their six-pound M-16 rifle. The largest man in the group, at least six-foot-five, had the group's hundred-odd-pound machine gun at his feet.

The tender was sending out four teams. This was the initial one, and it was important to get them started as soon as possible. The afternoon snow was already beginning to fall. The teams needed to get off the ship to vehicles where they would be ferried out to their site so they could set up camp before dark. The executive officer was looking around the room as he continued, "Take care of each other. Establish the sleeping tent at the locations we have chosen, then immediately set up the machine gun and communications. Stay warm. Never let your rifle get away from you and look out for each other!"

I looked down at the machine gun at the brute's feet. I knew it was designed to be broken into two roughly equal components. The gun was much too large for most men to wrestle with. I interrupted, "I want the women to carry the machine gun."

There was complete silence in the room.

Finally, the executive officer spoke. "Sir, the machine gun is too heavy for women to carry!"

"If they are part of the team, they can do the hardest work. I'll be watching. No man is to carry even one of those machine guns." I turned and left the compartment.

The commanding officer found me within ten minutes. "You can't make that rule!"

I looked at Ralph and then moved without speaking to a porthole to watch the women begin to struggle down the long steel gangway that led to the boats that would take them ashore. The two of us knew each other well. He had done his duty by making the point that I was being unreasonable. He shrugged and left to manage the rest of the awesome responsibilities of his ship. The troops had already adjusted to my arbitrary demands. The two largest women in each team were each carrying half of a machine gun in their arms. The strongest men in the team were crowded in front and behind each of the women, the women's packs and the women's M-16s slung on their backs along with their own packs. The men's arms were free, but hidden, apparently supporting the women, guiding them safely down the gangway. As the team reached the boats I stepped out onto the flag bridge so I could be seen watching as the team loaded. Several of them glanced upward with hostility in their eyes. Perfect! Whatever arrangements they made when they were out of my sight, when they returned from two weeks of being miserable, from being frightened and freezing, the men on those teams were never going to begin any conversation by saying that the women had been weaker.

Two weeks later, when each team returned, the strongest women were in the center, each carrying half a machine gun. Each member smartly saluted the colors and the quarterdeck before laying below. There was never a mention below decks about weakness, only wondering why the Soviets had yet to send any patrols even though we were only a few hundred miles from their borders, along with stories about the cold of the frozen night, the wild of Alaska, and how close the stars seemed to be.

A week passed and another opportunity blew up. A high wind. One that nearly killed us. In order to avoid despoiling the Izembek National Wildlife Refuge, we had been using a large, heavy barge to collect our garbage and other trash. We had rented the barge and had a tug haul it a thousand miles over from Anchorage. The barge had been tied off to the starboard side of the repair ship. This arrangement worked for a couple of days, but shortly after dusk one evening, the wind began shifting around the compass and building. The barge began rolling in the building sea and bumping against the side of the repair ship. As the wind continued to pick up, the barge would surge downwind until the lines snapped it back against the side of the ship. Soon the bumps had become bangs. The wind was now in excess of fifty knots. Before we fully realized our danger, it was too late to tie the barge off more tightly. The force of the wind on the barge was much stronger than the heaving from any number of sailors we could get on the barge securing lines.

Suddenly someone reported we were taking on water in a berthing area below the ship's waterline. We found that the side of our ship had been caved in for nine or ten yards by the action of the barge. Someone yelled, "Cut it loose!" Other crew members took up that call and several of the more aggressive ones rushed toward the barge lines with axes.

I knew permitting several tons of oily waste loose upon the Alaska fisheries industries and an unlighted killer metal barge to be driven pell-mell ahead of the wind through anchored fishing boats was definitely a terrible idea. I stopped any action to sever our tie to the barge. In a few minutes one of the officers came up with the idea to radio for the tug that had accompanied the barge to come alongside while the tender was conducting damage-control measures below decks (thirteen hundred people can do many more than two things at a time).

Within an hour, the tug had manhandled the barge off to a protected part of the bay and the CO and I had found places in the affected compartment where we could watch the ship team begin repairs. We both wanted to be near the action, he to observe how his people were performing while I wanted the crew to realize I too was physically at risk. I had also noticed something in the confusion of the damage-control team getting into place and was curious to see how it would play out. The compartment was partially full of water, and at the moment the sump pumps that had been dropped in were slowly losing their battle against the incoming seepage of seawater. The crew was still wedging mattresses into the long crack that had formed in the hull. Those mattresses were held in place and against sea pressure by shoring, thick precut wooden beams pre-staged throughout the ship. Water seeped in around the mattresses until welded steel could replace the white ticking. Ship's company welders had already begun at one end of the split in the hull. One team was welding plate, and the next was welding angle iron that would hold the plate in place. It would all be backed up with wooden shoring. It would be expected to hold until we got back to the calm waters of San Diego. We had nineteen welders on board. Their challenge would be fatigue and hypothermia, because they were welding in cold, cold water up to their thighs or chests. Within fifteen minutes it was obvious that the damage-control team had the problem well in hand, the water level had stopped rising, and the captain went topside to manage the safety of the ship in the intense weather conditions. I leaned back in a corner and adjusted my foul weather jacket around my neck.

Nine hours later, one very wet welder finished the angle iron on the final plate that overlapped the end of the tear in the metal hull. The pumps in the compartment were now making real progress. The compartment would be probably be nearly dry within the hour. Most of the damage-control team had been secured, including almost all the welders. Although a series of red devil blowers had been noisily sucking through the forward hatch all night, the air in the compartment was still foul from welding fumes. The ship had secured from "Flooding!" several hours before. There weren't that many people left in a compartment that only a few hours previously had been a beehive of activity. There were only five of us left at the scene. The rest had dragged themselves off to bed. The one welder making the final bead was an ironman. He had been there from the beginning. Two other welders, also part of the team that had initially reported to the compartment, were sitting exhaustedly on a section of unused shoring. The final sailor in the compartment was the welding supervisor, a senior chief who I knew was virulently antiwomen, so much so that he only had permitted one woman welder to ever qualify under him.

The final welder extinguished his torch and in the sudden silence his supervisor put his hand on his shoulder. "Son, I thought we were going to lose this f—g ship last night." There was real emotion in his voice. "I never seen anyone work this long since I was your age." He looked down at the welder's soaking wet dungarees below the leather apron. "And you must have been freezing." He half turned toward me, his hand still on the welder's shoulder, "I am going to get the admiral to give you some sort of medal."

And the welder pushed the heavy full face mask up and back, a shank of her dirty blond hair escaping, her high-pitched voice saying, "Thanks, senior chief."

Three months after we had returned to San Diego, the unmarried pregnancy rate on board the tender had plummeted from 11 percent to less than half a percent and a higher percentage of women than men were qualified in the key shipboard team roles. The following year, during the Gulf War, the ship was recognized by General Schwarzkopf as the finest repair ship in the fleet. On the return trip, the captain had a crusty old woman relieve a crusty old man as the senior enlisted person on the USS McKee. As Captain Schlichter was often heard to say, "Some of the best men on my ship are women."

Humans resist change. Tenaciously. They may not necessarily have a good reason. They may not have any rationale. But the fear of uncertainty often keeps humans stuck in their ancestors' emotional ruts. Stress can lever them out and up. Stress stretches the seams of established relationships and wrinkles the social fabric. Rather than battering against the bulwarks, stress tends to pry up a social barrier enough to provide an opportunity for a bit of good to wiggle past.

Faced with a situation of rampant sexual harassment and a high unwed pregnancy rate, I deliberately used real-world dangers in a remote corner of the world to force men to accept women as their peers and to simultaneously drive women to accept the challenge to behave more responsibly. Once the principles were welded in place, the ship's performance outpaced all others' in the fleet.

13 ★ BULLIES ARE NOT LEADERS

LEADERSHIP ISN'T EVERYONE'S CUP OF TEA; most people have enough on their plates in striving to be good managers. Consequently, there are never enough leaders to fill even the few essential billets. And while you may have a number of exceptional men and women, it is difficult to ensure that all the executive team is kept equally aware of everything. Any organization worth belonging to is normally over-tasked. Which means that things may be a bit uneven across the same organization. Everything may be fine in the kitchen even when a problem is abrew in the basement. So how do you keep abreast of it all?

I once was an admiral in charge of a large military organization headquartered in San Diego. As one of the perks of the role, a relatively junior employee was assigned to me as a gofer ("go for"). The assistant drove the official car when I was making calls, helped my administrative assistants handle my social schedule, and was generally available around the office. The job was obviously not nearly as dirty, demanding, or time-consuming as practically every other assignment in the Navy, especially since I was frequently absent from headquarters at sea or on travel and the gofer did not accompany me and had few duties during those periods. Thus, the role was a perk reserved for a sailor who had performed extraordinarily well in an afloat role and whose supervisors believed he deserved a "break" from his normal duties. Since it was a perk, the assignment was limited to no more than six months, so it didn't impact the sailor's normal career progress. The sailor in this case study was an electrician. In the two years I held my San Diego role, five or six different outstanding performers were gofers for me.

Given the background of the gofer role, imagine my surprise toward the end of my tour when I got a hand-printed letter from prison ("correctional custody unit" in Navy lingo). It was signed by the electrician gofer. He wrote that he had been in jail for nearly four weeks. It was less than four days before the last opportunity to appeal his prison sentence passed. He asked if I would come see him. The letter provided no other details. I checked the postmark. His deadline to appeal was today.

I had no idea what to do, but there was no time for indecision. I asked my senior enlisted advisor to accompany me in order to have a second set of ears. The two of us immediately set off for the prison. After some bureaucratic delays, we were sitting in a visiting room listening to my ex-driver's soft voice.

After working with me, the sailor had returned to his assigned ship. In the two years he had previously served on board that ship, he had always been evaluated as the best in his specialty. These high grades were significant, for while middle rankings may sometimes be assigned just to complete the rating form, the very top grades are reserved to justify accelerated promotions (higher salaries in less time) as well as special training opportunities. High grades are therefore awarded only after a great deal of thought and are always reviewed by the chain of command.

Within a few months after his return to the ship, the electrician had re-established his prominence within his group, regained his top rating, and felt secure enough to be married. His wife had been another Navy electrician. Since his career was going so well, they agreed she would leave the Navy and quit working as soon they were married, with the intention of becoming pregnant and raising their child. At the age of twenty-three, for the first time in his life, the electrician felt in control of his life.

And then, since he was now a married man and recognized as one of the very best sailors in a crew of more than fourteen hundred, he decided it was time to address a minor complication that had been bothering him for some time.

We are concerned in the defense industry that individuals do not abuse drugs. In order to counterbalance social and peer pressure in the age groups of most of our sailors and to ensure a problem never gains even a foothold, we have for decades periodically, randomly, and without notice required urine samples of everyone. The sample is then spectrographically tested for all drugs, including marijuana. As the testing has proven to be amazingly accurate (the residue of one smoked marijuana cigarette can be detected thirty days after the match was scratched), people have used lots of innovative ways to avoid detection, including such things as buying clean urine and keeping it in a rubber pouch next to their stomachs, etc. To defeat such efforts, there is a rigid process established, such as detailed records and a second person needing to physically observe each and every person providing the urine sample.

Ick! I know. It isn't a particularly genteel process. But military service life frequently involves rough methods, and the drug sampling process has proven to be successful, reducing drug use from more than 50 percent during the height of the tie-dyed days of the 1960s to only those few tenths of a percent of people who in general have other, larger problems.

Anyway, returning to our five-foot-five-inch, 110-pound electrician sailor, the problem he was ready to now confront was that he was shy, painfully so. In fact, he was one of those individuals that was unable to urinate when someone was watching him. This made it difficult for him to provide a properly monitored urine sample.

I will save you some Google time. The medical term is paruresis and it is a well-recognized condition, or at least it should have been. But I get ahead of my story. In the past our sailor had solved the problem whenever his number came up by drinking gallons of water until the pressure in his bladder overcame his involuntary muscle control. Of course, our shy sailor had to sit around for several hours, missing work and undergoing the gibes of his shipmates—groups tend to be impatient with people who are different—until nature acted, and the pain of bladder pressure, as many of you probably know, is exceptionally sharp.

He finally decided he would seek help and, like a good sailor, began asking for that assistance up his chain of command. I was later told that everyone at the bottom of the chain was sympathetic. Most already had heard of his problem, and, as we have noted, he had a particularly good professional reputation. He was referred to a psychologist on the ship for counseling. That's where his problems began. The doctor saw him several times and advised him he could do nothing. Quack! Quack!

The sailor was now nearing the top of the chain. He decided that the next time he had to provide a sample, in order not to waste working time he would ask the ship's doctor to insert a catheter up his penis!

Now for those of you males who may not have experienced this particular medical process, I will certify to you that this process is NOT painless! I can't even imagine how distasteful it would be if I were shy! Nevertheless, our electrician truly desired the Navy as a career. The senior enlisted man on his ship promised to provide that option.

You might wonder how nurturing these "senior authorities" were to the well-being of one of their best performers, one who had formally requested help. If the first doctor wasn't able to help, why didn't they find the electrician a better doctor—someone more knowledgeable— who might even have bothered to use Google or a medical equivalent? I had the same reaction. Sitting at the jail that day I was also becoming concerned. Daylight was fleeting and if I were going to overrule the commanding officer of a major fleet unit, not a routine action, I can assure you, I had only about an hour left in which to decide to do so. I urged the sailor to speed up his story.

A few weeks after our electrician had alerted everyone to his problem, it was again time for "all sailors whose social security number ends in four" to provide a urine sample. The shy sailor's number was four and he reported to sick bay for the special medical assistance that had been arranged. Unfortunately, no one there, including the doctor, seemed to recall the agreement. When the sailor proceeded up the chain of command and reached the ship's top enlisted man, he was told the senior authority had changed his mind. The top enlisted man said he "didn't want to establish a bad precedent."

There is no garble, misunderstanding, or mistype here. The "senior authority" apparently thought having a glass pipe shoved up his penis was so much fun everyone would be soon asking to do it! I directed my senior enlisted assistant to call and speak to his peer. The man acknowledged it had happened as reported.

So the top enlisted man on that ship had ordered the shy sailor to provide a urine sample the good ol' American way, with somebody watching, and the paruresis electrician had said he would try, but he knew he couldn't.

The top dog pointed out this was "direct disobedience of an order," a significant offense in any military, and one the conviction for which carried with a punishment much more severe than that which was specified for drug use! From that point on the gears of the military justice system had ground swiftly. The sailor was that day charged with the new offense and assigned an attorney for his defense. He drew a lawyer for whom this case was the new attorney's first post-law-school effort. The attorney asked his client if he had disobeyed an order. Our electrician had always been painfully, literally honest. He allowed as how he guessed he had.

His attorney pled him guilty and asked the ship's captain for mercy.

The Navy psychologist submitted an affidavit stating that he had examined the sailor several times and "found no medical or mental reason for his condition." The ship's senior enlisted man, the ship's captain's right hand man, said (the second quote of his I have no trouble remembering), "I've got over a thousand guys here; we can't be concerned about one."

With that comment, made nearly a month before, our electrician had been sentenced by the ship's captain to the maximum possible punishment in that court: six months in jail and a stiff fine. As a result of the fine, his pregnant wife had been unable to pay the rent on their first apartment, had been evicted, and had gone home to live with her parents while her husband went to jail.

While my assistant verified the rest of his story with a couple of calls, I used my seniority to bludgeon the system into releasing the sailor. It wasn't pretty and I didn't cross all the legal Ts, but "pretty" hadn't gotten the shy electrician in jail, either.

The case still angers me today:

> The man asked people he trusted for help. They failed him.
> He tried to find someone in the organization to care. No one did.
> He was denied justice. No one stepped up and stepped in.

A good man sat, his head shaved, in a cell for four weeks, wondering if a postcard to me would be viewed as too presumptuous.

I invited the ship's captain and his senior enlisted advisor to both retire and leave the Navy.

Leaders truly care about people. I always find it astounding to discover how few managers actually have empathy for those for whom they have so much responsibility. This case study is but one wrenching example of the low standard some organizations observe. In practically every organization you have people who should *never* have gotten to any position of authority. They make "people are our most important asset" a scorned platitude rather than a key slogan. Leaders without empathy are grit in the team's gears. Cast them out—like uprooted dying weeds—to shrivel in the sun.

14 ★ A CONSPIRACY OF SILENCE

JOHN LEHMAN, PRESIDENT REAGAN'S SECRETARY of the Navy during the 1980s, recently published a book (*Oceans Ventured*, W. W. Norton, 2018) discussing the maritime security strategy that he promoted while he was secretary. In his book (p. 96) he comments: "In early years of the strategy, while we modernized the fleet a certain amount of bluff was necessary."

Even for those not involved at the time, that specific note might prompt someone to ask three questions:

- Just how much bluff are we talking about?
- Was any sort of net assessment made before the maritime strategy was launched?
- What really happened?

Well, the maritime strategy was a whole box full of bluff. And what actually occurred makes for an interesting case study.

It was a while ago, so it is necessary to set the stage. It also involves providing some background as the situation had developed over some time. Our own submarine force had become more and more secretive in their war against the Soviets. As a result, nonsubmariners simply assumed all submarines were ineffective. That was a deadly mistake.

This misconception began in the 1970s and stretched into the 1980s. During this period, with the singular exception of the submarine force, the Vietnam War had been the primary focus of the Navy. This had been true for nearly thirty years, throughout the 1950s, '60s, and '70s. The war lasted longer than the Beatles' careers. It had finally wound down in 1975 while the Cold War was slipping into its own third decade.

One deep breath in time and President Reagan had been elected and was installing a coalition of young hawks in his administration. There were some initial embarrassing missteps in the military area, several of them involving the Navy. Nevertheless, Secretary Lehman of the Navy still had Reagan's ear and was working hard to make himself and the Navy a unique success story. He had an angle! While the Soviets had a grand nuclear force and an overwhelming army in Europe, their surface navy was not nearly as strong as ours. Was that an American opportunity? Lehman believed that if the Soviets refrained from a nuclear strike, it was possible to conventionally defeat the Soviets through the application of carrier air power.

This was the essence of Secretary Lehman's maritime strategy. He has written that it was conceived in 1977 by him, Graham Clayton (former Secretary of the Navy), Bing West (a former U.S. Marine), and Jim Woolsey (later to be the Undersecretary of the Navy and still later director of the CIA) at a dinner at the Black Pearl Restaurant in Newport. The concept was relatively simple. In the event of hostilities with the Soviet Union, rather than waiting to move our carriers forward until our submarines could beat down the Soviet attack submarine threat, American carrier forces in the Atlantic would immediately push north. From positions close to Russia they would attack the Soviet submarine bases on the Kola Peninsula and dispatch the several dozen long-range A-6 bombers on board the carriers to support the Air Force on the German central front. In the Pacific, naval carrier–led forces would immediately steam toward Vladivostok and support amphibious landings to threaten the city.

The maritime concept thus emphasized the flexibility of the aircraft carriers. It envisioned conventional weapon tactical strikes that would turn the tide of any hot war dramatically in favor of the United States. It also contained, however, two strategic shortfalls, one acknowledged and one ignored. Both were deadly. The shortfall made clear was that the Navy needed to double the number of carriers and air wings (add twelve new carriers) and that this powerful force would have to be procured at the expense of the Air Force or would require billions of new monies for defense. The missing carriers were a major part of the "bluff."

Why do I say this was a deadly error? Because even if Congress were willing to spend the money, it would still take fifteen years to build this force. Even more important than this practical aspect, no matter how many carriers we built, they could never get near the Russian shore! The secretary had wrongly assumed the powerful Soviet submarine force was toothless!

Unfortunately, after President Reagan was elected, the maritime plan's false principles were quickly included into the National War Plan!

How was such a gross error made?

Because too few people knew any better. A conspiracy of silence existed about the poor state of antisubmarine warfare (ASW) in the Navy. It was wrong, widespread, and potentially disastrous. Why?

Ground warfare had been with us for centuries and was well understood. The same was true for surface ship battles, which were essentially armor engagements in flat terrain. Air warfare engagements, although relatedly new at the time, were easy to analyze; there are few mountains in the air.

But unlike the United States, the Soviet Union had not focused their military effort on the air threat. They had deliberately built a military asymmetric to the American one. The Russians were a land army that wished to control Europe. Their navy was not carriers, but an enormous submarine fleet intended to prevent the American fleets from even attempting amphibious landings on their shores. And, by the way, the undersea environment was extraordinarily difficult to measure and model.

Perhaps it wasn't terribly surprising that the Lehman group that had been having drinks at the Black Pearl restaurant hadn't known much about ASW. One might have expected more. We had almost lost two world wars because of submarines, and both times we had been saved by signals intelligence, not by destroyers. And the first nuclear submarine in the world, the USS *Nautilus* (SSN 571), had been commissioned not far from Newport in September 1954 and ever since had been unchallenged at sea. Even worse, the Naval War College was located a few blocks away in Newport. Why were so many so ignorant about ASW?

First of all, as Jack Nicholson yelled in *A Few Good Men*, "You can't handle the truth!" Submarines had been an emotional issue for our Navy for nearly a century. It had been touch-and-go to counter German submarines during the Battle for Britain during World War I. Between the wars the Germans had managed to rebuild a submarine force that, until we broke their Enigma code, had driven the U.S. Atlantic Fleet to distraction during World War II. After the end of the Vietnam War, the Soviet Union had the largest submarine force in the world, numbering more than three hundred. We had only half that number. The American ability to counter the Soviet force was, at the very best, dubious. How effectively U.S. Cold War forces could dispatch the Soviet submarine force was the great unknown. I had been one of the hotshot submarine commanders tasked to do so and I certainly had expected that a war would be a one-way mission that didn't include a ticket home. Our carriers would be waiting for our submarines to decimate the four-to-one advantage. You were expected to press your attacks until the law of averages and enemy waters caught up with you.

Second, while the American submarine force had been focused on the Soviet Union, for a quarter-century John Lehman and the rest of the nonsubmarine part of the Navy had been fighting in Vietnam and worrying about resisting the Air Force. They hadn't spent long years submerged gazing at icy shorelines and listening to Russian call signs while internalizing the strengths and weaknesses of the Soviet Union. The Vietnam War had just ended two years earlier. To see how the concept of competition with the Air Force permeates his thinking, see p. 92 of his book. In a passage describing why Secretary Lehman took the submarine force training principles to apply to the Navy air community, he states, "The submarine community was in very good shape, as . . . it had never lost its focus on the threat from the Soviet Navy *and the Air Force*" (italics mine).

The third prop under the silence conspiracy was the big picture. The U.S. Navy does a great deal more than conduct warfighting against a peer competitor. And although nuclear submarines are efficient killers, they cannot even begin to do the complete range of missions our country needs a navy to perform. Submarines do not carry large numbers of troops like amphibians, don't manage large area reconnaissance as well as airplanes, have trouble rescuing people at sea, cannot be easily rearmed in foul weather, and most of all don't look menacing. These are all characteristics a world-class naval power must have. Therefore, through the 1950s, '60s, and '70s, while big-deck aircraft carriers were being assaulted by the supporters of the Air Force, the Navy brass had their hands full fighting off this daily conceptual assault. Admirals were not much interested in even talking about any Navy ship's susceptibility to submarines, and anyone in the Navy who brought the subject up was considered disloyal.

Finally, there was a practical problem. Because of manpower constraints, there were few nuclear submariners available to spread the gospel about the dramatic new capabilities that speed and endurance had provided nuclear submarines. Consequently, the rest of the Navy was not getting accurate feedback about how the advent of nuclear submarines had drastically changed the ASW threat. The Navy was building submarines as fast as we could to stay ahead of the Soviets. Even with special officer accession programs, that meant there were no nuclear submariners available to spend tours ashore at Newport talking to their peers over a beer after work, or in a postgraduate school in Monterey, California, or anywhere else in the Navy. For example, eighteen of my first twenty years were spent assigned to submarines, and each submarine deployment in the Pacific was thirteen months, with turnarounds of less than six months. Moreover, no experienced nuclear submariners were available to fill the schoolhouses or even provide inputs to fleets or staffs. The only ASW information anyone at the schools was getting was from ne'er-do-wells who had been cashiered from submarines or those diesel veterans Admiral Rickover had never accepted into the nuclear program. The latter two groups were not the best sources on nuclear submarine capabilities.

At the same time, wargaming had gained great credibility in the Navy. As I have previously noted, wargaming can solve some problems, but in this case, it provided the Navy with an opportunity to push their ASW problem under the rug. Modeling is susceptible to mathematical manipulation. People make rules, mathematicians write algorithms to express those relationships, data is inserted, a computer analyzes, lights blink, and results print out. Most people simply read the bottom of the page. Garbage in, garbage out. Very few ever take the time to understand the assumptions, much less check the math by which the assumptions have been reduced to zeros and ones.

A war game is thus vulnerable to having ill-understood rules, sometimes made by individuals who don't realize the implications of particular assumptions (and perhaps every now and then a computer rule is written or manipulated by someone with evil in his or her soul).

Because of all the peer pressure, it should come as no surprise that the war games and exercises the Navy was doing during the 1960s and '70s tended to demonstrate again and again that U.S. nuclear submarines (the ones that looked and performed very much like Soviet submarines), while perhaps the best effective force against Soviet submarines and being preferentially funded by American presidents, were evaluated by Navy (nonsubmarine) admirals as not worth a tinker's damn against U.S. Navy surface ships. In fact, it was as if each U.S. Navy surface ship and carrier wore some sort of invisibility cloak that warded off undersea danger.

I served four years as an executive officer on board an attack submarine and commanded a sister attack submarine for another four years. I must have done a hundred exercises against surface ships. I knew how vulnerable they were and also how the reported results of each encounter had been skewed. I didn't have a Wiccan background, but I did have one in system analysis and mathematics. I spent my spare time reading, computing, and unwinding the underlying war-gaming assumptions that created the nonsensical exercise results. I uncovered astounding errors in the game rules: wizardry that altered the laws of physics; false assumptions about submarine torpedoes to ensure they would never acquire the surface targets; enchanted invisibility cloaks; and plain deceit. But no matter how much I explained and complained, my submarine was always considered toothless against U.S. surface forces.

If years of bad data are permitted to accumulate, summarized into generalities, and provided up to senior levels, it is not long before the erroneous results become the brick and mortar of someone's equally flawed *plan*.

One afternoon in Honolulu, in a heated discussion about the bias of antisubmarine war gaming, in which I (a midlevel captain) was the only non-admiral in the room, the argument segued into a conversation about the recent National War Plan change. It was my first introduction to the new maritime strategy. It had become a recent major revision to the existing highly classified War Plan. In the Pacific, in the event of conventional conflict with the Soviet Union, instead of now waiting for several weeks for the U.S. nuclear submarine force to attrite the Soviet submarine forces near the major Russian port of Vladivostok, the American aircraft carriers would immediately take the war to the Soviets. This would be done by a combined American and Japanese fleet, accompanied by an immense antisubmarine screen of ships and an umbrella of strike aircraft intended to sweep in and land Marines.

As one of the two submariners in the room, I knew this would be certain death. Since no one else was choosing to speak up, I did. "It is a dumb plan. It will be suicide for the tens of thousands of young men and women on board those carriers and amphibs. There is a reason we let our submarines go in first."

The hum of conversation in the room immediately died. Fifteen admirals turned to look at me. From his seat on the top row, the commander in chief of the Pacific Fleet, Adm. Bob Foley, made a temple with his hands underneath his chin and said, "Dave, are you saying the Soviet Pacific submarine force could stop a force of five carriers, fifty-five antisubmarine warfare ships, and nearly three hundred antisubmarine warfare airplanes?"

"Admiral. The Soviets have more than a hundred submarines in Vladivostok alone. They would kick our butts!" His face was without expression. I raised the stakes. "If you don't believe me, let's check it out at sea. Give me only seven of the oldest submarines in your fleet. Send your five-carrier force against me and I will realize your worst fears."

Two months later, neutral controllers on board every ship, we played the largest at-sea war game ever done. My forces were still labeled "Orange" and I had agreed in advance to some restrictive metrics (very reluctantly to one). In return, I had been permitted to provide my own secret aggressive tactical guidance to each of my submarines. I also personally directed and operated them as if I were a Soviet commander defending the homeland. When the bell rang at the end of two weeks, it was as if my mismatched submarine group had been welded from the bluest of steels, with my promised consequences.

It was only later that I fully appreciated Adm. Bob Foley's wisdom. He must have strongly believed or at least suspected that the maritime strategy was fatally flawed. But no matter the plan's shortcomings, Admiral Foley could not directly criticize it while simultaneously keeping the trust of the secretary and his boss, the president of the United States. But he could manipulate the zeal of a foolish Navy captain.

After the exercise, Admiral Foley tasked one of the junior flag officers who had commanded one of the strike forces, a known favorite of both President Reagan and John Lehman, to be the Pentagon briefer. The admiral presented the results as favorably as he could. He noted the U.S. forces had made a great effort, an amazing number of sorties had been flown, tens of thousands of sonobuoys had been

Admiral Bob Foley. He revised a flawed National War Plan so deftly there was no cry to find anyone to blame. He went on to become President Reagan's assistant secretary of energy for defense programs. *U.S. Navy*

dropped, etc., etc., etc., and only about a dozen of the hundreds of ships were lost (only all the carriers, oilers, and most of the anti-air-warfare ships).

He left unvoiced two points:

1. There were no airplanes left to protect the amphibious forces. The landing could not have succeeded.
2. There were no kills of Orange submarines.

The National War Plan was immediately revised.

There is a related postscript. For several years I wondered what might have happened if Admiral Foley had not so quickly located a scapegoat and so carefully planned his "acceptable briefer." What if the United States had gone to war before the War Plan was changed? If we had followed it, both of America's largest fleets would have certainly been destroyed! Over the next year I made a point to speak to many of the admirals who had been in key billets during the few months this plan was in effect. The reaction of most of them was, "We [my peers and I] spoke about it as soon as the plan hit the street. We knew it would cost us all or most of the carriers. We were never going to do it. If war with the Soviet Union became imminent, we were going to go with the old plan [that immediately inserted U.S. submarines into the contested areas near Murmansk and Vladivostok and relied upon them to attrite the Russian submarines before exposing the carriers]."

Each time a conversation went down this path I only prayed for a poker face as I silently nodded. But inside I was thinking, "Oh really?" How was that going to work? In the event of war with the Soviet Union, you were *not* going to execute the War Plan that the president and all your subordinate commands had been so carefully planning? As things got tense, *then* you were going to dial up the Oval Office and explain you were having second thoughts?

But that's what most of them told me. Except for Admiral Foley and the Atlantic Fleet commander, Adm. Harry Train. And my old boss, Vice Adm. Bud Kauderer, who I now suspect had been in cahoots with Admiral Foley from the beginning and had been instrumental in suckering me into the meeting. He knew me so well.

A final question and closing thought. Are you surprised by how such an important issue was disguised by silence? How big a "conspiracy" can be? How few of the supposed leaders were actually leaders?

Never, ever let foolishness stand, no matter how high it originates. If something is wrong, it is wrong. Don't condemn yourself to live the rest of your life with regrets.

15 ★ RED FLAGS AND WARNINGS

MY WIFE AND I ONCE TOOK A SUMMER TRAIN from Rome through Tuscany to Florence. Before we reached our destination, I understood why Van Gogh had painted all those sunflowers. The fields of waving gold mesmerize. It is nearly impossible to see any imperfections in the rest of the Italian countryside. This has happened to me before. This is a case study about when I failed to notice some human weeds growing right under my nose.

At the time I was responsible for about ten thousand people on forty or fifty different ships and detachments. The units were spread along the coast of California from the desert of San Diego north eight hundred miles to where the redwoods meet the churning cold waters of Oregon. The men and women heading these organizations were collectively some of the best America had to offer. Everyone involved had spent years working long hours to keep America's nuclear submarines at sea.

I knew best the seventeen officers who reported directly to me at my headquarters in San Diego. These were my major commanders, all with serious responsibilities. Each was a senior Navy captain with more than twenty years of service. In addition, I routinely interacted with thousands of other officers and enlisted, and often with their spouses and significant others.

In addition to the training and maintenance of submarines, my role enabled me to take on other professional objectives. As one of these, I was determined to significantly reduce the number of suicides among our young submariners. In the years before I had taken charge, the number of suicides in the submarine force had gradually risen to an unsettling number. I was convinced this situation could be turned around. Consequently, we had put in place policies that amplified sailors' awareness of what they could do to help their susceptible shipmates. I had personally put the power of my office behind some new policies. With the new information and our public emphasis, we hadn't had a suicide in nearly eighteen months. Until the previous week in Vallejo.

All suicides are tragic events. The initial report I had received on this incident had been no different. The young man had been in charge of accounting and disbursing for his submarine. There had previously been rumors of possible small cash shortages in his unit. A new commander had recently taken over the ship and had requested functional assistance from my overall organization in conducting an independent review of his ship's financial records. The audit had been scheduled to commence last Monday. The police autopsy placed the time of death as late Sunday evening. Evidently someone had not been sufficiently careful with government money.

It was the afternoon of the following Thursday. I was reading about a maintenance issue and looked up at a noise in the hallway outside my San Diego office. I recognized an officer attached to the same ship as last week's suicide. It was surprising to see him here. Vallejo was six or seven hundred miles away. Lt. Cdr. John Jolliffe and my chief of staff were arguing about the fact that John didn't have a scheduled appointment to see me. I removed my glasses, rubbed my eyes, and motioned both of them in.

As a precautionary measure, when an untoward event involving Navy people takes place, the Navy also does its own investigation— in addition to the one run by the police—the extra investigation is directed by "line" officers. While the latter don't have nearly the same experience as trained law enforcement professionals, naval officers have a better understanding of the culture of the Navy. The naval officers also have security clearances, which may be vital to gaining access to all the information in the submarine force. Pragmatically, the naval officers also tend to get a little better cooperation when, in the interests of justice, they need to wander far afield, in this particular case from the stark question of whether or not the young officer had been murdered (a fact already determined by the police) to the question of why he had killed himself. I don't recall whether or not I had heard that Lieutenant Commander Jolliffe had been assigned to do the investigation, but evidently he had.

John walked into the office and placed a large stack of paper on my large mahogany desk. He then stood stiffly at attention alongside my in-basket and reported, "The new commanding officer appointed me as the investigating officer. I'm done. That's a copy of the report I will turn in when I fly back to Vallejo tonight. [He] killed himself. He was probably afraid of what the audit team might find. I've also talked to your head financial guy who is right now wrapping up their report. They have discovered two thousand dollars missing and several unexplained purchases."

I offered him coffee and a chair and waved the chief of staff to go back to his other duties.

John refused both and continued with words he had obviously carefully rehearsed. "My report is accurate. However, if you really want to know what really killed [him], you need to select someone else to do more interviews. The next time, assign an officer senior to the last commanding officer."

The sun from the window behind my desk made his eyes squint. I agreed that I would assign a new investigator and again asked him to sit.

John's shoulders slumped and the emotional strain he was under became apparent. Investigating a suicide is absolutely gut-wrenching. The investigator always gets caught up in the despair the victim was experiencing. John abruptly sat down, balancing his body on the forward edge of the chair for a second and then pushed himself back into the deep leather. It turned out that his new commanding officer did not know John had used his personal funds to fly down to talk to me or that John was delivering me a raw copy of the investigation. We talked for a long time about how conditions had been on board his ship under the last commanding officer. The sun slowly marched across my office rug and disappeared below the window ledge.

When John, who would in the future be himself promoted to admiral, left my headquarters, so did my very senior deputy. They were both booked on the next plane to San Francisco. My deputy was tasked to reinvestigate the suicide. Concurrently my staff began a memory and record search. Had we missed any red flags?

No one could immediately recall anything. We had evaluated this particular submarine as low average, not among the best, but not unsafe; if we went to war, we expected it to survive, but probably it would get a below-average number of kills. We sifted through what we knew about the thirty-plus submarines in our organization. Let's see, the leadership team (senior three or four officers) on that unit had been together for about two years. Had anything unusual happened. . . ?

Well, they had certainly experienced an ill run of luck! In fact, as I thought about it, I could remember several unusual people events.

The first one that came to mind was when one of the most experienced department heads, the engineer officer, had falsified a ship's record. It had certainly been a bizarre incident. Before he had left work one day, the engineer had written down, as he did each evening, what he wanted done during the night shift.

Several weeks later, someone pointed out to the engineer that his order, as written, could have permitted a technically incorrect action that under some circumstances might have proven very costly. A large, expensive piece of equipment might have broken. The issue was now moot, because the men had recognized the error and chosen the technically correct method of conducting the maintenance. The equipment had been subsequently inspected and determined to be operating without problems.

Unfortunately, instead of self-reporting his error and accepting a little criticism, several months later, the very day before the annual engineering inspection, the engineer had crossed out the incorrect order in the old record book and written in a replacement order, as if the change had been made contemporaneously with events. And he did this in front of a witness!

This was a clear violation of our integrity standards. There was no question about the facts. Nor the inappropriateness. Our organization can't employ people who are unable to accept responsibility for their own errors. Now the man had to be replaced. Strange incident. I had never seen or heard of another one like it. And yet I didn't stop to think at the time about the unseen pressures that must be boiling on that ship to cause the department head to commit the one act guaranteed to get him fired the day before an inspection team came on board that would undoubtedly discover it!

One.

What else had happened in that unit? Well, now we didn't have to think long before recalling that the previous commanding officer had recommended that the ship's number two not be promoted any higher. The commanding officer had said his executive officer was just not a take-charge person and "didn't keep mistakes from happening." It was a serious accusation. It meant the executive officer had lost his boss's confidence. It had meant that after fifteen years of an impressive record and extensive training, the executive officer was finished. Good thing this doesn't happen very often. Just this once in our thirty-four ships!

We have millions of dollars invested in each of these unique individuals at this point. Which doesn't mean that everyone who reaches the executive officer level is fit to take the next step up in responsibility. Some are not. And the commanding officer is the one who is best placed to make this judgment.

One of my peers at this time was a friend of that particular executive officer. The other admiral called and asked me to speak to his friend to see if I could determine what had gone wrong. To see if he possibly could be fixed. It was an unusual request because the executive officer was essentially four supervisory levels below me in our organization, but admirals tend to treat each other with deference. By the time I finished my little inquiry, I had spoken to each supervisor between me and the individual and had spent more than an hour with the subject himself. In our conversation we covered a wide range of subjects. I was trying to get a feel for him, his family, what he wanted out of life, if anything particular was troubling him, possible personal problems, etc. I have done literally thousands of one-on-one personnel interviews.

This man was clearly a personable guy. Bright. Interested in his career. God-fearing. Involved in the community. Candid. Not terribly confident. Told me his problems were completely of his own doing. Told me he had made too many errors and had been unable to support the commanding officer as well as he should have. Told me that he was probably not cut out for the responsibility he currently had and was looking forward to leaving the submarine force and entering into a less demanding line of work.

I decided there was not much to be done about this unfortunate situation. Each level of supervision had assured me the executive officer wasn't doing his job. He himself admitted he wasn't fit. It was unusual, but . . . I informed my admiral-friend of my findings and figuratively dusted my hands. When I was a very young leader I had observed how easy it was to destroy nearly anyone's self-confidence. I had learned that real leadership was helping men and women to bravely take their weaknesses in hand and face the unknown. When had I forgotten about the fragility of egos and how easy it was to ruin someone's mirror?

Two.

Funny, in the glare created by the light of the suicide, when I thought back about the two years that most of the ship's wardroom had been together, there had been some sort of flaw in nearly every officer on board that particular ship, except of course for the commanding officer. In fact, there had been another incident where one of the relatively senior officers on board had experienced what we had euphemistically at the time referred to as an "integrity problem."

This time it had been another one of the senior officers on board: the operations officer. He was completing his three-year tour of duty on board the submarine and was about to be transferred to a desirable job overseas. During the relieving process, his relief found that three years of a key training record were all falsely backdated. The records were clearly bogus. Each entry had even been made with the same pen!

Well, uncompleted training is one problem, and not entirely the operations officer's own, as there were several people on the ship who should have noticed the training was not being conducted, including the commanding and executive officers, for both were required to document their own monthly personal study. But forging records is something else entirely. We severed the Navy's relationship with the officer. Permanently.

When actions are irreconcilable, there has to be a deeper problem. Each of these people problems should have been a red rocket exploding in the air telling us, specifically telling me, there was something seriously wrong within the command.

Three.

Our human relations department reminded me of another incident.

One of the young officers on board that particular ship had simply chosen not to go to work one morning. Instead of continuing across Tennessee Street to the Mare Island Causeway, where he was expected to participate in a vital work project that began one Monday, he turned his motorcycle left and rode two hundred miles to his mother's house. He had remained there in seclusion a week before returning. He gave no reason nor offered any excuse. I had never seen a young officer behave this irresponsibly. His records indicated he was exceptional, an honor graduate from one of the top five schools in the country and previously a solid performer. It was so odd that I had him flown to San Diego to talk to me.

He told me he had made a mistake in choosing nuclear submarines as a career. This was his first ship and he had realized during the past six months that he didn't have the personal drive to succeed in our demanding line of work. He didn't believe he was adequately contributing to the organization, so there was no sense in staying. Too bad, I had thought. Impressive young man. Damn shame he has so little self-confidence. We initiated procedures to terminate his relationship with the Navy.

In the Navy, officers' actions reflect directly on the commanding officer. When officers vote with their feet, they are flooding the ballot box. I knew that intellectually. I had forgotten it pragmatically. I wonder where that man is today?

Four.

And finally, a friend called. He had heard we had been asking questions about a specific individual, the former commanding officer: "You know that guy once worked for a friend of mine. He was the number two on that ship. Their submarine had the most terrible incident. I never heard anything quite like it. Their engineer, their number three, attempted suicide by drinking a glass of acid." I heard my friend gulp over the phone. "I can't imagine how much it must have hurt!"

He paused for a second as if he were recalling and I mentally shook my head. He probably used the chemicals from the ship, which are terribly powerful and must have started burning even before they were past his lips! How could anyone be so distraught as to even consider it? My friend's words continued tumbling into my ear, ". . . really too bad. I met him once or twice. Extremely bright fellow. Well liked. Top performer. Truly one of the submarine force's stars; why do people like that even consider suicide? He seemed like such a positive person. I saw him after they had released him from the psychiatric ward and he recovered as much as he ever will. His sister is my wife's cousin. You have to lean really close to hear him. Doing something with woodworking now. He says he is just sorry he hadn't been good enough to adequately support his boss. You know the acid burned his vocal cords."

Five—at least—and how many other unknowns had he destroyed in his previous assignments?

When my deputy's investigation arrived, there was a lot of evidence that the previous commanding officer had been promoted well past his level of competence, but still well short of his wife's expectations. The commanding officer possessed none of the easy personal competence that lets juniors and seniors understand that while minor mistakes are never desired, they are also not the end of the world.

The previous commanding officer and his wife had never missed the opportunity to privately or publicly criticize any of his officer's missteps, even imagined ones. As one consequence, his officers would do nearly anything to avoid the commanding officer's (and his wife's) vituperative tongues. The officers were relatively inexperienced and lacked confidence. Most were unsure. They were essentially trying their wings. Should anyone have been surprised that the young officers on this ship lacked self-confidence?

And what about the problem that had finally caused us to finally look closely at the ship? The investigation found the previous commanding officer had pressured the young officer to buy unapproved items. Especially bright shiny ones that would make the commander's change of command appear impressive. The young man had informed his boss several times that this was wrong. But the young man had finally yielded to the commanding officer's pressure and made the purchases in his own name.

And then a new commander came on board, found the numbers didn't add up, the young man's explanations inadequate, and called for an audit team.

For years I and his immediate boss—distracted by daily detritus—had ignored numerous red flags. This was particularly galling because I had personally suffered from the same sort of predatory leadership when I had been young—and had damned my commanding officer's supervisors at the time for being so dismissive—yet I had failed to recognize an even worse case! My lack of attention sent a young man home to his mother in a box. Don't you make the same mistake.

It doesn't matter what supervisory rules, regulations, or tripwires exist if the leaders are asleep.

16 ★ TOUGH BUT UNFAIR

TOUGH BUT FAIR. Have you ever admired this particular phrase? Ever considered how nice it might be to see this label ascribed to you? Perhaps affixed beneath your picture in some Who's Who? Is the description accurate? Or are you like Frank, a peer of mine just downright mean?

When I was fresh out of college, every one of us aspired to be leaders. I can still recall my own hesitant beginnings. We were like turtles scuttling out of the hatching nest toward the safety of the sea. I still remember my fears. I recall the overwhelming desire to be considered "cool." The "tough but fair" reputation appeared to be a particularly desirable label to achieve. I yearned to be personally worthy of a tag so . . . adult. If I were considered *tough but fair*, I would certainly no longer have to worry about someone thinking I was still wet behind the ears, no siree! Troublemakers would sit down and shut up when someone *tough but fair* showed up. That sort of person was not going to be led down the primrose path by any damn goldbricker. *Tough but fair* leaders were nobody's fool.

Young men and women grasping for leadership positions are not dumb, but they have such a terrible fear of being thought a fool, they certainly may appear stupid. They recognize that no college or academy, no matter how highly respected, adequately prepares anyone to lead. Therefore, on the first morning a young manager reports to his or her new job, the fear of being embarrassed is often topmost in the new manager's mind. And it is so easy to believe that some of the workers are lying in wait to "put one over" on you. I mean, we all attended high school, didn't we? Didn't we talk about how dumb some teacher was? Didn't we pull tricks on him? Or her? Didn't you play sports with someone who was continually putting the coach down? In my peer group of young officers, Frank was the one who always did that. Except he didn't make fun of the coach. He made fun of our weakest link, the person in our group having the most difficulty with the assigned task. Over the years he became infamous for his biting comments.

Did you want people even possibly laughing behind your back? Or would you rather be known as *tough but fair*?

There is a great temptation to adopt the tough but fair technique, isn't there? And the first job is the precise time when new managers learn techniques they will tend to use, for good and for bad, over the rest of their lives. I have watched, supervised, and reviewed the records of literally thousands of managers and leaders. If there is one truth I have learned, it has to do with *tough but fair* leaders. While they may appear to be quite good, if you delve into those who worked for them, you will find they trashed a lot of good people. They cost the organization invaluable resources because they were using a harsh exterior to hide their own areas of incompetence.

"Tough" people don't handle uncertainty well. They have difficulty understanding or adapting to complex situations. They don't assimilate new data as rapidly as others. The "tough" guys and gals I have met usually permitted their personal fears to stymie their own development. Which unfortunately is not meant to imply that such leaders and managers don't or won't frequently succeed. Life is often not fair. Not only do harsh leaders often look good to their bosses, people respond to fear and intimidation, just as did the Egyptian slaves. For limited periods, people work faster under a whip.

On the other hand, over extended periods, I have observed, unequivocally, that a good leader can get better results without stooping to being "tough." Rather than trying to learn from those tough-but-fair role models, you should avoid such individuals as if they had heavy colds. "Tough" is a crutch for those managers and leaders who haven't worked at learning leadership skills or are simply in situations over their heads.

But let us assume you are no longer in the initial years of your first job and therefore long past any juvenile longings for the *tough but fair* sobriquet.

As you are probably already aware, the key to job success is actually handed to every leader on a silver tray: because people try.

People are a gregarious, tribal-oriented, chauvinistic, peer-affected species. This means that the path forward is not gained by stoking up the pressure on them, but rather by constantly reassessing what you as the leader can do to help your steeds put the optimum strain on the traces. The good leader is constantly (re)evaluating, observing, and sorting his people. People need to be assigned jobs they can perform. Because of our human nature, an individual will literally work himself to death trying to meet expectations. People will spend extra time at work, think about the problem during their off hours, lose sleep, and give up their personal life. They will try harder than we deserve.

We need to worry about what we are asking others to do. If we assign impossible tasks to individuals, we will eventually find the employee dead with a gun in his mouth, suddenly charged with spousal abuse, the victim of a one-car accident late at night, or, if we are very lucky, only admitted to a hospital with "general exhaustion."

When any one of these happens, if he pauses at all, the *tough but fair* leader will turn tiredly to his mental chalkboard and chalk up yet another disaster to the fragilities of the deplorable humans she has to work with. The good leader, however, will have earlier recognized the mismatch of talent to task and shifted the specific individual to a job she could perform. The change will probably have been accomplished over the visceral objections of both the employee and his intermediate supervisors, all of whom professed to be worried about the employee's feelings, perceptions, future career, and the needs of the organization. Don't worry. They are all wrong. The shift is not only possibly life-saving for the individual, it also will open up an opportunity for some previously underappreciated employee to blossom.

While ignorance on the *tough but fair* manager's part might be an excuse, real stories are often worse, and it is time to circle back to my friend Frank. I once was asked to provide a leader from my organization to shift to Frank's command. His engineer officer had attempted suicide and his organization was in extremis. Although Frank and I had begun as peers, I was now running a larger organization. I had developed good people I could spare. One man was even particularly well suited to fill the engineer officer position Frank needed. The individual had worked for me for two years and in that time had demonstrated excellent growth as well as exceptional performance. He was interested in the billet Frank had open and it was time in his career for my man to move on to new challenges.

Subsequently, months later I was surprised when I heard through the grapevine that my replacement engineer officer had been unable to handle the pressure of his new job. After working for Frank less than a year, he reportedly had broken down emotionally. He was recovering in the same health facility as his predecessor.

Some years later, out of the blue, I received a tearful Christmas Eve telephone call from the man's wife. She asked why I had sacrificed her husband. I expressed surprise. Her voice got more insistent. Surely I must have known I was sending her husband into a veritable lion's den. I must have known that Frank had a richly deserved reputation of being *tough but fair*. That Frank would sacrifice anyone for his own success. And that her husband was not the second engineer officer that had broken down while working for Frank, but the third in three years. "Everyone knew the problem was not the job or the men, but the man in charge!"

Up until that moment, I hadn't spared a moment to recall Frank's true nature. After our initial training tour together, I had usually been in a different geographical area from him and been busy beating back the wolves from my own sled. Her call properly took me to task. I stopped what I was doing and listened. Then I reflected and made a few telephone calls of my own. Within a few hours, I had a clear picture. Frank had spent a professional lifetime trashing people to cover up his own shortcomings. The engineer's wife was correct. Her husband had been unfairly destroyed.

Some time later, Dame Fortune finally cast her runes and Frank was forced to resign from the Navy. It was for a different reason, but rough justice is often still justice.

Those who manage by being tough but fair ignore the fact that nearly everyone is trying to do their best. A leader's primary function is to assign people to jobs they can do or tasks they can successfully grow into. You also must do the hard work of reassigning those who are in the wrong roles. If you aren't doing all three, you are only pretending to be a leader.

17 ★ DIRTBAGS

JEFF BEZOS, THE CEO OF AMAZON, talks about making decisions when you "have conviction even if there is no consensus" and getting to "consensus with questions." He has a line that goes, "I know we disagree on this, but will you gamble with me on it? Disagree and commit?" He believes his success depends on quality decisions made in this way. I agree that sometimes the facts are as difficult to agree upon as the future. The bottom line is that often a leader has to act decisively before everyone is fully comfortable and certainly long before consensus is reached. Such action involves the essence of leadership.

To set the scene for this case study, my headquarters at the time was in Japan. Our role was to keep the United States' attack submarines gnawing at the Soviet Union's throat. To facilitate this task, several organizations worked for me, including a submarine repair facility located in Guam. The repair group was quite capable and included a large ship (a submarine tender) that held about fourteen hundred workers, machine shops, laboratories, and everything needed to repair a submarine. There was also a drydock moored at a nearby pier. The repair ship was commanded by a senior Navy captain with twenty-five years of experience. For the purposes of this case study, his name was Bill.

Now, selection to the next rank in the submarine force depends on demonstrating your skill in a few specific billets. You can be the finest instructor at the Naval Academy and never make it. You have to go through the jobs the submarine force values, and Bill was in one of those jobs. While the chances of Bill being selected for admiral may have been ten thousand to one when he started out as an ensign, and narrowed down to a thousand to one after his first twenty years in the Navy, from where he was now, the odds of him getting at least one wide gold stripe on his sleeve had risen to about fifty-fifty.

In addition to the decades of exceptional performance that had earned him his current chance and major responsibility, Bill had two unique arrows in his skills quiver. First, he was personally very charming. He was a noted virtuoso with the violin and could turn any social event into an evening everyone would always remember. If that weren't enough to grease the remainder of his short slide to the top, he had recently been selected to command that ship to replace another senior officer whom I had fired for shortcomings! Firing someone at that level is a rare event. It was an embarrassment to the submarine force and had only been done reluctantly. Since the force had just gone through the emotional trauma of publicly embarrassing one of our own, one so near the top, I—and everyone else—was willing to give Bill a very long leash and lots of credit for even mediocre work!

At the time this story took place, Bill's ship was moored in Guam. Although I was fifteen hundred miles away from Bill, and often more from some of my other commanding officers who might be in port somewhere in Asia or Africa, I spoke every week to each of them. If I couldn't see them, I at least wanted to routinely hear the voice of everyone who worked for me. I wanted to hear how he or she sounded.

Routine conversations to keep your boss both updated and comfortable are a good and normal practice. You don't want every ring-a-ding between subordinate and boss to presage a problem. If that is your practice, it won't be too long before you have trained your boss to be frowning before he picks up the phone.

As Bill and I were talking this one particular day, I heard the wail of an ambulance in the background. The siren sounded as if it passed fairly close to his ship before it faded into the background. I knew the repair facility was in a fairly remote section of Guam, and I had never before heard traffic noise on any of our calls. I idly asked, "What was that, Bill?"

"Nothing much," the voice at the other end of our satellite link reported. "Some guy—a real dirtbag who never manages to do anything right—didn't wear his gas mask while painting. He collapsed from the fumes. Serves him right. We're taking him to the hospital pretty much as a precaution."

"Ummmm," I brightly replied. I subsequently steered the conversation to the next item I had jotted down on my three-by-five card: one of the submarine commanding officers had reported the facility was having problems in getting scheduled work out on time from the tender's hydraulic shop. This was one of the recurring difficulties Bill had been having. He was trying to balance his mission of repairing submarines with the need to do periodic work on his own thousand-foot-long

tender. The conflict would soon be in our rearview mirror as the tender completed its six-month self-overhaul project.

Later that evening I was reviewing the day with my spouse, as I am
required to do by clause 206 of our standard modern marriage agreement. While I recapitulated for Linda what had happened that day,
I was subconsciously thinking of the times I have personally ridden
in an ambulance. As we talked I was reflecting that while I've been
hospitalized more than my fair share, I've only been transported in an
ambulance twice. Never on a lark. Both times were when my life was
hanging by a thread.

Wonder why someone called an ambulance for the "dirtbag"? Who
had been that frightened? How close had the sailor been to dying? Life
at sea is incredibly dangerous and sometimes those risks have to be
accepted. But had we endangered someone in port? Letting someone
under your supervision be needlessly harmed is inexcusable.

I called Bill the next morning and asked for an investigation of the
incident to be performed and forwarded to me for review. "OK, no
problem. I will get someone right on it."

Time for a short digression. Senior military people reading this
will know that anyone who runs an organization as large as Bill's
routinely initiates and internally reviews investigations like the one
I asked for. But it was a major breach of protocol for me to direct
him to do this investigation and another infraction to ask for it to be
sent to me. Yet I did. Why? I don't know. I can't remember what had
caused my confidence in Bill's judgment to begin to flake. Possibly
I was hearing other reports that made me think he wasn't paying
attention to detail. Maybe I was factoring in the conversation I had
had with his wife the last time I had visited them in Guam when she
shared with me that she was worried that Bill might be drinking too
much. I don't recall. I knew I probably shouldn't have directed that
action. But he didn't object! And even more importantly, he didn't
tell me that he had already started an investigation. Both of these
facts bothered me.

A number of days passed. I was involved in submarine operations
from Africa to Japan. My attention had been diverted to other problems. Then we received a call on our whistle-blower anonymous tip
line. Every large organization has a similar system. They are set up so
that anyone can call in and their identity will be protected by a third

party. The caller said, "Things are 'f—d up' in Guam!" No specifics. No details. Five words.

I suddenly realized it had been nearly a week since I had asked for an investigation of the "dirtbag" and there was no appropriate stack of papers bound with a rubber band on my desk.

I immediately called Bill. He said everything was fine. In fact, the investigation was complete and he had reviewed it himself. He had read every page. Nothing untoward had been uncovered. He spoke for several minutes convincingly and knowledgeably about the incident. He then shifted to the status of the facility's current tasks. They were completing the self-refurbishment of the submarine tender spaces—the project they had been working on for the past six months—and he felt they were over the hump with respect to its interference with submarine repairs. Only the tender painting remained. He assured me that the submarine commanding officer who had just left Guam would be the last one that would ever call me with complaints about delays. He said the tender had been working on three submarines but was going to temporarily suspend all work except on the tender and put a full-court press on the painting project for a solid five days. He expected to get each of the subs to sea on time during the next month. All good news. These submarines were the frontline defense of the United States in the Cold War with the Soviet Union! We needed them out there.

We terminated our call and I sat back and thought. Despite a great deal of very public and continuous advertising about the whistle-blower number, calls on that line were infrequent. Almost never, maybe one call in a calendar quarter, and inevitably it was a crank call from a drunk. It wasn't unusual to have a quarter go by with no call. Only one individual call most probably meant nothing. It certainly wasn't part of a trend. And only five words! I thought some more. I had a bad feeling. Why had I even told Bill to forward the investigation to me in the first place? Normally I would have trusted a senior captain's judgment. Why wasn't it already on my desk? If something bothered me enough before the whistle-blower call that was sufficient to order him to perform the investigation . . . what was I going to do now? And by the way, why hadn't Bill volunteered to forward it?

I redialed. "Bill, put that investigation on an airplane and have it delivered to me today. Shut down all work on your ship until I have reviewed it."

Another case study interruption. Having fourteen hundred repair experts sit on their butts while three submarines and a repair tender needed attention was not a good career decision for me. Especially since I had lately been on everyone's back about the need to get cracking on submarine work. It was going to become quickly known throughout the Pacific theater that work was being held up while a plane was flying (at what cost?) from Guam to the Naval Air Facility at Atsugi, Japan, and then my personal driver was going to have to thread his way through the bumper-to-bumper traffic to Yokosuka just so I could read a report, one that had already been read, reviewed, and approved by a competent authority. And Bill and I were the same rank. He was not the only person who was soon going to be looked at for selection to admiral. Lots of people were going to be asking questions about my judgment.

It took twenty more hours before the seven inches of paper were neatly stacked on my desk. To paraphrase the first forty pages (the summary), the investigation had concluded that one individual had violated several company rules and behaved irresponsibly. Doctors had subsequently determined that the subject individual had not been permanently physically harmed. The individual had admitted his fault.

Ho hum.

As Bill had been keeping me informed for several months, the tender had been sequentially refurbishing the ship. To do the work expeditiously, many crew members were involved in work they were not usually assigned (e.g., electricians were doing painting, etc.). Therefore, the organization had set up special training for everyone—no exceptions—in electrical safety, operation of portable power tools, painting, etc. The tender was especially proud of its plans and preparations. As proof of the crew's special effort and of the "dirtbag's" willful violations, the investigation included several inches of the published plans as well as the appropriate training attendance records for the thousand-odd employees.

Most of the facts seemed clear. The young man had picked up his painting equipment and left the central control point. His task was to paint a small windowless room three stories below the main or "weather" deck. Within twenty minutes he had come stumbling up to the weather deck looking drunk, short of breath, and with paint splashed all over his coveralls. Someone had seen him and tried to help him walk to a doctor but he had collapsed before they had gone twenty feet.

It appeared he had practically begged to be killed or to suffer permanent brain damage. A supervisor had seen him pick up a mask before he left a central area but the dummy had apparently discarded it as "too dirty" as soon as he was out of sight! There was even a signed statement in the investigation package in which the worker (the "dirtbag") acknowledged he had ignored several safety precautions, including that he knew mask-cleaning equipment was readily available.

The review by the Guam repair facility followed the standard format of determining facts, drawing opinions, and developing recommendations. It was an open-and-shut case. The facts supported the concept of a "dirtbag." I could tell by reading between the lines that the people in the organization believed they had behaved most professionally.

My chief of staff came into my office to tell me that various staff members were beginning to field calls from around the Pacific. Senior people on the Guam tender were more than a little bit irritated that I had even asked them to conduct an investigation. They were also professionally up in arms over the fact that I had stopped work. They were beginning to call their own friends around the Pacific Rim and asking, "When was work going to be restarted at the Guam facility?" It was merely a matter of time until one of my three admiral bosses called me.

I riffled the hundreds of pages of the investigation in my hands and decided I would have to read more than the executive summary. I began. Less than an inch in and the entire investigation began wobbling.

On several of the training attendance records, no matter what the date or the subject, the "sheets" were all signed by the same people in the same rough order. Had they all arrived in the training room in the same order on each training day? Had they all sat, like grade-school children, in the same seats? Had no one been busy elsewhere on the ship? Had no one been sick? Had the sign-up sheets been passed around the room each day in the same order? Or, after the "dirtbag" incident, had someone realized they were missing some records (whether or not the training had been conducted) and asked everyone to sign? I was becoming suspicious of the integrity of the investigation.

But then why did the "dirtbag" admit that it was all his fault? Why did he discard his air-fed mask? No matter how dirty the mask, he had to realize it was a lifesaver. I was tired. I ignored the possibility of more phone calls. I needed to walk, think, and sleep on the report. The tender would have to sit idle another day.

Later that evening I was explaining my uncertainties to my most critical audience (remember section 206 of the spousal agreement). My wife is not a physics major, and I was explaining that paint for metal walls is always oil-based so it will stretch and contract with the temperature changes in the ship. As the paint dries, it releases the chemicals that keep the paint fluid while it is in storage. Those chemicals are powerful volatile emollients and the paint is a fast-drying one. As the liquid is spread on the metal walls, the vapors literally roll off in waves.

Which is why, I explained to my spouse, we only applied this paint under carefully controlled conditions. We either used big blowers and ducting to create conditions that continuously flushed the entire volume of the room with fresh air or, more commonly, such as this case, where someone was working in an internal compartment down a few decks, the individual used a pressure-fed air mask. Managing the hoses, I told her, was actually a more difficult problem than managing the painting. Frequently there will be two dozen or more air hoses running through the same watertight door. When you try to move a single one it is difficult to identify the right one and not disturb someone else's from two decks below you. Concurrently, the hoses have to be suspended from the overhead by strong steel S-hooks so they won't be damaged or kinked, and the whole bundle is so heavy that by the time the hoses are arranged to just begin the job, the workers frequently feel as if they have already done a full day's work.

But the air hoses are absolutely necessary because painting with an oil-based paint is such a potentially dangerous job. In fact, given all the possibilities of different sizes of faces, beards, and other reasons a mask might become ill-fitting while working, in addition to incidents with the hoses and the air-fed masks, we have a firm safety precaution that no one is to paint alone.

As I was explaining this to my spouse, I realized that nowhere in the investigation, in the statements or in the pictures of the scene, had I seen any reference to the bundle of air hoses that should have been feeding air to the painters in the internal compartments. Nor had I seen a statement from the "dirtbag's" assistant. Damn! That was what had been bothering me! I made a call to one of my senior deputies to pack a bag and head to the airport. He had a rendezvous in Guam.

Within twenty-four hours I had a new set of facts.

The "dirtbag" had overslept and arrived at work late, for the third time that week. His supervisor had been justifiably angry. But rather than waste more time than he felt the problem rated, the supervisor had just reached into his job bag and assigned the "dirtbag" the most miserable job available: painting a small windowless room in the hottest part of the ship, down three levels in a space without ventilation. The supervisor had not assigned a helper precisely because he hadn't wanted to "punish" anyone else with a job that was so dirty, hot, and tough.

The "dirtbag" hadn't complained. He knew he deserved some sort of discipline for his tardiness. Since he had not attended any training, he hadn't known there was a prohibition against painting alone. It wasn't clear that the supervisor had realized he was violating several specific safety guidelines. The supervisor had also neither received nor done any training. Because of all the work on the submarines, the group had gotten a bit behind. The only training this particular team had participated in was to gather together in one room one day, pass around eight sheets—each labeled with a different subject—and have everyone sign to show that they had all attended.

"Anyone have any questions?"

"No? Class dismissed."

They didn't consider they had lied. The training had been scheduled. It just hadn't been worth a tinker's damn. It wasn't clear who had the bright idea of subsequently putting different dates on each of the attendance sheets to file with the investigation.

Even worse, since no one had done any effective training and none among them had ever painted as part of their normal professional duties, nobody had been forced to get smart enough to realize they had requisitioned the entirely wrong air mask system. The painting being done was with oil-based paint, where poisonous vapors are the problem, but they were using a mask system that only protected against particulates, which is the danger in water-based paints. There was thus nothing protecting their lungs and brains from the noxious vapors! The "dirtbag" was such a fast worker he had finished painting his entire job area in less than thirty minutes. With four walls blooming organic poisons, each unmasked breath must have been nearly equivalent to downing a shot of vodka every minute or so. It was a surprise he lasted twenty minutes.

It was a miracle he didn't die.

Why hadn't he complained? Remember, he didn't. He even signed a statement admitting the whole incident was his own fault.

I don't know for sure. But let me hypothesize. The "dirtbag" knew he wasn't pulling his weight. He was eighteen years old. He certainly didn't know the rules any better than anyone else in his section. He didn't know about organic emollients, much less about air-fed masks or the two-man rule. He certainly didn't know he might die; no eighteen-year-old suspects the possibility even exists.

That the victim doesn't know enough to complain doesn't ever mean anything! Much less imply that everything is under control. What would have happened if work on board the ship had not been suspended? Remember they were about to start five days of dedicated painting with a whole bunch of people using the wrong air mask system! Wonder who made that anonymous telephone call? I have always suspected it was the immediate supervisor once he realized how close he had come to killing someone, even if that individual was someone he considered a dirtbag.

The men and women on this tender thought they were good people working day and night to do the right thing for their country. Yet because of incompetent leadership, they nearly killed at least one person and, unless stopped, would have endangered many more.

In this case study the "problem" sailor turned out to be simply a confused eighteen-year-old. The real "dirtbags" were the managers who had failed to properly evaluate a potentially dangerous evolution. To compound management's faults, when the situation went south, the "dirtbags" slapped together an investigation to hide the problem and nearly killed many more shipmates.

Sometimes a leader has to take a risk well before he has all the data he or she would prefer.

18 ★ WHO IS RESPONSIBLE?

ON BOARD A SHIP, there should be no question who has the responsibility for every event.

During the Cold War, there was a particular protocol for attack submarine missions. If the submarine were to be given the approval to conduct covert operations, this permission needed to be granted by the president of the United States. This warrant was then specifically documented in a written record referred to as a "finding." At least part of the reason for this process was to maintain a record to demonstrate to Congress that the president was personally involved in deciding when covert operations were necessary and that lesser mortals in the executive branch were not running around willy-nilly granting approvals for operations that potentially posed political dangers for the United States.

Which is essentially what this case study is about: responsibility and accountability. When things go wrong, people often subsequently cast around for who was to blame. Sometimes there appears to be a question. That is a mistake. It is always the man in charge, always. I have often been in charge. I always held myself personally responsible for failure. That singular responsibility drives the person in charge to do what is necessary to ensure success. Let me give you an example.

I conducted operations under presidential "findings" on several occasions. These findings were invaluable. They gave us the flexibility to accomplish what American needed done. Unfortunately, as is true with nearly every bureaucratic system, sometimes minutiae became caught up in the process. In one particular case, the date my submarine was scheduled to get under way from San Diego had been used as part of the descriptor in the presidential finding. Which is normally a good thing. You want the submarine fully armed with all of its permissions the minute it goes to sea. And most commodores (i.e., my boss) were possibly not nearly as rigid as mine. It was, after all, only the first day of what was planned to be a thirteen-month deployment.

It had been a struggle to ready my ship for this particular deployment. A submarine needs both great people and great equipment. The late 1970s were a down cycle for all the military services in recruiting. America's youth had not yet made their mental recovery from the double whammy of being lied to about Vietnam and then experiencing the Watergate scandal. To a few wayward young men, girls and the Grateful Dead had more appeal than years of duty on board nuclear-powered submarines. The Navy leadership was consequently having to sift through more people than usual to get an acceptable number of acceptable recruits. Crews numbered a bare, bare minimum, and working hours were noticeably longer during the few days (often less than thirty a year) that boats were in home port.

My immediate predecessor on board the ship had been comfortable with lower material standards than I believed appropriate and with a less aggressive operating approach. In fact, the previous commanding officer had been less demanding about lots of things. I spent my first four months in an upgrade mode. The crew had been working hard to meet the standards I was insisting upon. They weren't entirely happy, but they well understood that in their world I set the height of the bar.

I was now ready to steer our submarine back into the same exciting theater of operations against the Soviets that I had left less than a year earlier during my executive officer stint on board another submarine. I could now focus on refining our schedule. Immediately after leaving San Diego, we would conduct a three-week transit to Pearl Harbor during which we would execute a number of drills and exercises to familiarize everyone with their teams. Then there would be a short pit stop to pick up some last-minute supplies, green vegetables, and milk, followed by a three-week transit to station and the first of our three-month operations against the Soviets. But when I took a breath, I could already see there was a serious glitch. The schedulers had us getting under way on Friday, July 2, to match the date on the finding.

Why in the world would I get my tired crew under way on a late Friday just so that they could miss spending the most patriotic weekend of the year with their families? The Pacific Ocean is very wide. Simply by pushing up my transit speed by a smidgen, maybe a tick, my nuclear reactor wouldn't notice, but I could make up a couple of days in transit. Our ship was not scheduled to return until August 18 of the *next year*! That was the earliest day we might be back, and submarine deployments were often extended. My last submarine had been extended a month in her thirteen-month planned voyage. I had been busy and hadn't focused on this foolishness before. My fault, but on Monday of that week I decided this was crazy. I knew that given the engineering items that still needed to be done, my crew would be exhausted by Friday. I was not going to get under way with a tired crew. I went up to my boss's office to discuss this.

He informed me the Friday date was sacrosanct. This date was specified in the president's finding. He pointed out that I had not objected to that date until it was only a week away. He noted that if my ship didn't get under way on that specific date that I would be personally identified as deficient to the Chief of Naval Operations and the president of the United States. He also threatened that he would seek to have me replaced. He was *not* going to ask to change the date in the finding. Okay, his intent seemed clear. I gave his words some thought and then observed some of my crew members in their work. I continued these observations on Tuesday. I reflected on the fact that I was personally responsible for the performance of each and every one of these individuals. We had fixed the key material items but I was not about to get under way to proceed to sea with a number of my key people exhausted.

On Wednesday, I informed the commodore that I would be unable to get my ship under way on Friday. I would be fully prepared to do so on Monday, and asked him to have the president revise the finding. I had the executive officer direct the crew to take the weekend off to enjoy time with their spouses and significant others. Over the next few days, the commodore was apparently unable to convince his seniors to relieve me. It turned out that it was easier to have the president initial a pen-and-ink change to the finding.

Maybe not the best start to a voyage, but since two years later I would be in the White House situation room briefing the ship and crew's accomplishments, and accepting a Presidential Award on their behalf, it didn't work out all bad.

I have always believed that a ship's commanding officer is responsible for everything that takes place on board his command—no matter who has supposedly directed what—and one time, when the president of the United States was theoretically involved, I had the opportunity to live my words.

19 ★ STOP THE BLEEDING

HOW DO YOU DEAL WITH terrible situations?

Aggressively.

A disaster never occurs because of only one or two errors. That may be what the participants say. It may even be what the immediate supervisors think. False. Never happens. Thousands of years of tragic mistakes say otherwise. An incident doesn't happen until four or five consecutive mistakes click into place. Not one. Not two. A really bad event requires four or five miscues, sometimes even more. By the time a fire breaks out, a ship runs aground, or an explosion takes place, several supervisors have already had their opportunity to save the situation. It is well past time to take decisive action.

Most managers still won't recognize the situation for what it is. They simply will add one "never" to what Peter Pan might have given Wendy for directions and establish their own new law of three "Neverlands." No matter how long terrible indicators may have existed, supervisors *never* accept that the situation is as awful as it is. When directed to address the problems, they *never* look deep enough and they *never* take adequate action to root out all the rot.

I will give you an example. This one is from business.

I once was working in a growing company headquartered near Washington, DC. We were focused on marketing, so we needed to minimize other corporate costs. For example, instead of having a full-time corporate human relations professional of the appropriate seniority, we had a relatively junior full-time professional at headquarters and a much more qualified consultant, the latter a woman named Margo Parker. Margo served us in a multitude of roles, including augmenting our Human Relations staff. When she had worked full-time, Margo had been an exceptional performer, actually serving as the first female VP at a major defense company. Now she commuted from her retirement home in Missouri.

Margo consulted on several levels for the organization and sat on other companies' boards of directors as well. Although I was ostensibly her boss, I knew that was only true on paper. At the time of this case

Ralph Crosby. General manager of the B-2 bomber program and more senior roles. West Point Graduate. One of the best leaders I ever served with. *Courtesy of Ralph Crosby*

study, she and I were still in the peer phase of feeling each other out. In our highly competitive company, we both knew we were operating in a serious dog-eat-dog world. Decisions always involved hundreds of millions of dollars and thousands of jobs. Talent was weighed against tradition and the value of old-boy networks. Making new friends was not done casually or without serious calculation. True allies were invaluable.

Late one morning, my cell phone rang. I was at headquarters. The display showed Margo's number. It was Tuesday. I knew Margo had planned to be on the West Coast for a board meeting and had planned to stop by one of our nearby units if she had the time. She was then headed home for an Easter weekend reunion with her grandchildren. We had a unit in California the CEO of which had recently been replaced while I was away on another assignment. Consequently, I had not met the new CEO. Margo had planned to stop by and see if there was anything the new CEO needed.

"Dave, I think you need to get out here as soon as you can. If you get here by early tomorrow, I will stay and meet you at the airport with Mary [the local CEO's human relations vice president]."

"Why do I need to come?"

"Because Mary has records that seem to indicate that our new CEO has been embezzling since the day he first walked in the door. She says she started keeping records after he sexually harassed her."

"I will send you a text with my arrival time at the LA airport."

Mistakes are often made in selecting people for new jobs. People are put into positions they can't handle, or new responsibilities unexpectedly expose hidden flaws. The question is: What do you do when trouble breaks the surface? Are you also a follower of the law of the three nevers? When I arrived, I reviewed the data. It was obvious our new married CEO had a casual and undocumented approach to mixing his own and our company's resources. More seriously, I believed our whistle-blower's accusation that he had made unwanted advances to her and at least one other employee. And while Mary didn't recognize the violation, it became apparent from our conversation that the CEO was also breaking state law by surreptitiously recording telephone and office conversations with his peers, his superiors, and his customers. If all this weren't enough, from my quick review it looked like he was off to a terrible business start. Instead of making the $5 million in profit he had promised for his first quarter, he had instead lost $7 million!

Margo and I sat down and talked to him about "whistle-blower" complaints we had received. It quickly became evident he was sure he was smarter than both of us, and was confident he could explain everything. He had lunch brought in for the three of us so that he could command our full attention and weave a pattern of lies around our shoulders. Unfortunately for him, in the four months he had been there, he had destroyed company morale and had already lost the support of his immediate staff. No one had warned him about what we already knew. He had no idea that Margo had already spent the previous two days on site talking to his immediate staff or that I had spent three hours at the LA airport that morning reviewing her notes and speaking to the "whistle-blower," his administrative assistant.

After a couple of hours, the CEO had unknowingly lied himself into a corner with contradictory statements. I left the room and had my Washington administrative assistant make a fake call to give me an excuse to fly back to headquarters. I didn't say anything to anyone in California about what I thought about the problems we had found. The unwitting CEO drove Margo and me to the local airport.

I had already decided on the appropriate immediate action but I needed to take the precautionary step of setting a bureaucratic backfire. I had not found, vetted, or hired this particular CEO. I knew that at his level of seniority he had to have a patron in our organization. I needed to quickly find that mentor, present him or her with the evidence, give him or her some face-saving reason to let me kill the loser, and invite the patron to be part of the solution. This is often a necessary step in business. Without it, nothing would happen in the company and the value of our California organization would quickly dissipate.

Fortunately, it was a long flight from LA to DC, and the California employees had been discouraged by my unexplained exit, particularly when the CEO had held an "all hands" meeting immediately after returning from the airport to announce that he had the corporation's "full faith and confidence" and "would deal very harshly" with anyone who tried any further whistle-blower tactics on him. During the four and a half hours I was in the air, several key California employees had placed their resumes on common job-hunting sites. One of the people who had done so was the head of the California engineering department. This particular woman had just received national recognition. Organizations always think their supervisors know everything and look down with x-ray vision. Our California unit had judged corporate's tepid response to their situation and were already voting with their feet.

But the unexpected first-quarter operating loss was what made my argument easy when I finally located the sponsor. Businesspeople hate red ink! The CEO's mentor was more than ready to sever any association!

Within a few hours I was back on a plane headed west to spend Easter weekend in California. I had decided I would need to serve as the temporary CEO. I called Margo and asked her to return to help after her grandchildren located their Easter eggs. On Friday, I evicted the current occupant from his office and from our premises, leaving his contract settlement as details for Margo and our attorneys.

Over that weekend, I personally met with each of the eleven vice presidents. The executives and I did a deep dive on all the financials. Unfortunately, the first-quarter loss was real. They were also engaged in several more projects that would inevitably produce losses. Some other projects had suspect long-term payoffs. We needed to stop the cash burn for the company to survive in order to have time to alter direction. We needed to stop the bleeding.

The executives weren't dumb. If you carefully listened to each one, there was a clear solution. The team was simply reluctant to make tough decisions, and the way forward did not involve all of them. The company's overhead was much too high! The next Monday I fired seven of the vice presidents. On Tuesday, we consolidated from 368 to 224 employees, cancelled the plan to institute a new business software program, and issued plans to close the three subsidiary sites. I projected that we would recover the first-quarter losses by the end of the year. Step one was completed. The head of engineering pulled her resume off the web and Margo farmed out the severance agreements to a local team of attorneys.

But any competent executive could have taken those broad steps. The CEO hadn't, but I had fired him for his shortcomings. The next aspect that needed addressing was his casual approach to company money. What example had that set for the rest of the company? Was it automatically corrected when he was booted out the door? And what about the implications of casual sex? There were at least still two nevers to go.

When you have one problem that trips your alarm bells, always look further. Many people back off because they find details that are uncomfortable.

With respect to the CEO's financial miscues, they could never have occurred if the local CFO (chief financial officer) and his assistants had been competent. In the case of the local CFO, he had negotiated a special "deal" in which he maintained a residence in a different state and commuted to work only when he thought it was necessary. I called him up and told him to stay home; his services were no longer necessary. That closed one barn door. I would deal with that long-term fallout later. Right now I felt like the morality of the company needed immediate shoring up.

According to our whistle-blower, the previous CEO had taken several mistresses in the workforce. The whistle-blower had reportedly started keeping her diary on the financial transgressions after the new CEO began the same process. The whistle-blower seemed credible. I also suspected the head of second-shift production had made a play for the CEO. I know the woman had approached me during Easter weekend to ask if I wanted to have a drink with her. What else was going on here?

Margo and I made a visit to talk to the previous CEO. It did nothing more than put him on notice. He had a different moral framework (he actually had been a rock star before he went to college) and had millions of dollars at stake from his buyout. When queried, though, he was not reluctant to list the women from our company he had or was currently dating. We then followed our noses. Sometimes Margo and I split up discussions by sex or by seniority. Within a couple of days, we weren't sure we would ever know how many women had engaged in sex with the rock star CEO, but we knew that several in the workforce had participated in gatherings that included nudity. In fact, we quickly were in possession of pictures.

Now, if the workforce felt that no one was interested in enforcing the basics of sexual morality, and the CEO, who was paid oodles more money than anyone else, couldn't keep money in the right boxes, and the people in finance (the checkers) were incompetent, who else was simply not paying attention to making money? We did a second weeding of people by sexual appetite and thought about how we could best use the time we had bought to reorient them and focus everyone on a common successful future that kept everyone's job.

I decided the answer was to spend time on details. The company was in the business of producing semispecialty items that cost $400 to $2 million per unit. We had a catalogue of products anyone could order. We would modify a product (for a price) for a serious customer. Since there was a high degree of specialization involved, I suspected we might have lost some grasp on what our margins were on all items. It had been a while since anyone had taken the business down to the capacitors and bolts and priced it back up.

So we began a serious review of the top 400 (actually 358) products that we sold, building the value of each item up, component by component, step by step, adding cost by cost. To each we added appropriate surcharges for marketing, corporate contributions, etc. After several weeks we could show data for each individual item three years back and make projections one year forward. When done this way, some numbers fell directly into our laps, such as that we were selling one of our competitors a product at more than a million dollars below our own raw component cost!

For several components we also found the repair costs over the past three years had been more than the purchase price. This drove home to the staff the requirement for better quality in our manufacturing. We quickly instituted quality tracking on each product we didn't discontinue. The staff then let this information publicly drive our internal investment decisions.

After several months of effort, I had my hand-picked successor in place and I could return to DC. Margo and some trusted others (specifically Gen. Mike Hough and Tom Darcy) stopped by to give my successor an occasional hand. I periodically returned every couple of weeks for reviews and finally formally turned over the reins when I was positive that good habits were in place.

The organization subsequently grew and was successful.

When a problem occurs, don't paper it over. Do the necessary investigation until you understand the root causes and then fix them! Don't rely on a situation to fix itself. Happily-ever-after only happens in romance novels and Neverland.

20 ★ LEADERSHIP AND SQUARE PEGS

PEOPLE SOMETIMES PAINFULLY CLAW themselves into assignments for which they are fundamentally ill-suited. Once such a person is positioned, no matter how obvious the misfit, few supervisors are eager to involve themselves in the messy business of rectifying the error. Nevertheless, it must be done! The downsides of the situation are devastating to the unit and the individual. A good leader constantly re-evaluates and re-sorts his people and tasks.

There are reasons we aspire to be leaders. There is nothing as great as the satisfaction in helping individuals and an organization grow and succeed. At the same time, there are also onerous tasks only the leader can perform. One is the reassignment of square pegs who have been mistakenly assigned to round holes. Moving someone out of the wrong slot is akin to doing a drug or alcohol confrontation. Many executives find this process so uncomfortable they invent excuses to always be elsewhere. They don't want to get their hands messy dealing with emotions. The intervention may save the individual's life, but don't ever believe that the alcoholic (or the abused spouse, or anyone else involved) will be grateful, now or anytime in the future. Rather than a surprise bequest in a future will, plan on a surplus of drama. Nevertheless, the work is critical. Let me describe what once happened when I screwed it up.

Some time ago I had an individual working for me whom I will call Ron. Ron was a popular person, one of those genuine individuals who makes friends easily, immediately, and forever. Although we were in a military organization and relative rank normally defines working relationships, in this case I had unique qualifications that Ron did not, so although Ron was older and senior to me in rank, he nevertheless worked for me.

This rank inversion could have been awkward, but as I have established, Ron was an upbeat individual and his natural charm made our relationship work. His spouse had a similar personality and quickly became one of my wife's best friends. Ron had been present when I reported on board and everyone was of the opinion that he was an exceptional manager. He certainly was smart. And fun to be with after work.

I quickly found that Ron could do any specific job I gave him. Which was good, for we were in a very demanding environment. On the other hand, it was vexing that we always seemed to have problems in Ron's area of responsibility—each time a different issue—that I often had to finally take in hand and fix myself. It took me six months to realize that although Ron could solve practically any task, he could handle only one or two—maybe three—concerns at any one particular time.

Ron's job was like many senior management roles. It required him to simultaneously keep twenty to thirty balls in the air until specific manpower was available to address a particular difficulty, until a solution was evident, or until it was simply the appropriate time to launch an all-out corrective effort. Unfortunately, he seemed incapable of prioritizing. Instead, Ron assigned equal precedence to each item. He would almost randomly select one to dither upon, spending insufficient time to finding a solution, before he loosened his grip on that one ball, whereupon it would float back into the mass of revolving, colored spheres that hovered around him like a swarm of friendly bees. My friend would then pluck another from the ever-increasing number of orbs, and instead of regarding it as the old friend they had nearly now all become, look almost surprised to find it once again in his hands. It was maddening to watch!

It took me six months to recognize the depth of Ron's problem and almost a similar period to determine that none of my recommendations as to how to deal with his ever-increasing workload were going to make the slightest difference in his behavior. It wasn't that he wasn't listening or trying. He couldn't change. He was smart as a whip but had difficulty dealing with uncertainty. When I finally recognized the absoluteness of his limits, I arranged a transfer for Ron to an easier job elsewhere. I did it as gently as possible. I did it without any fanfare so that he and his wife could hold their heads up in our common community. Perhaps I did it that way to be easy on me, so I would not have to look directly into his eyes and tell my friend precisely why I believed he could never be a successful senior manager.

If I had been more experienced at the time, I would have recognized that while his new job was only half as demanding, it was still going to be a disaster. Ron was still going to have to deal with uncertainty. Unless he transformed himself, he was going to need to completely change careers. When he didn't do either, he had his first heart attack at the youthful age of thirty-two. After a long convalescence, he finally became a professor at a university. He now has an intellectual career without demanding timelines or a myriad of problems. He was a much happier individual. He is still alive and going strong in his late seventies.

Many leaders may not recognize these people issues as their problems. It is true that employees often build a work failure situation for themselves: by struggling to a level they eventually (or more quickly) find too rarefying; by permitting pressure from spouses, peers, and relatives to propel them to begin to assault mountains they can't possibly ever climb. But even if they can't do the assigned job, perhaps they can do another in the organization. In my experience none of these individuals were sullen, obnoxious, or even had acne when they were young. Each tried. Each was eager. Each worked terribly hard. And finding the right slot for these people—or moving them completely out of the organization—avoided emotional or physical breakdowns as well as degradations in the mission.

By the way, you are probably not going to have any assistance in doing the right thing. Until disaster visited, I could never find an ally to agree to help me make an overachiever understand they were in over their head. At the same time, I have never had any square peg make it easy to help them shuffle from a round hole to a more suitable role. Each time it was all up to me. The individuals were distraught when I told them they were hurting us. None of them recognized they would live longer, be happier, and probably make more money working in a square hole job. Sometimes I had the emotional strength to follow through and make the right decision. Other times, honestly, I crumbled. It was always easier to do nothing.

Sometimes the individual survived. Other times they had single-car accidents late at night. When that happens, you are going to be asked to go to the funerals and give the eulogies. I at least did that. I stood on the stage by the flag-draped coffin to remind myself not to wimp out the next time.

The memories of your people mistakes never retire or fade.

21 ★ INTEGRITY

INTEGRITY REMAINS THE GOLDEN RULE of any relationship or organization. Observing any lower standard has a terrible cost.

Integrity and good management normally walk into the workplace hand-in-hand. The importance of not stealing, cheating, or telling lies seems obvious. A good leader understands the essence of the concept and the importance of ensuring that the principle is observed.

At the same time, we cannot pretend to be naive. Pathological liars, as well as cheats and thieves, can be successful. In the U.S. Navy, I once worked for a compulsive liar. He flourished principally because he was so rare, a liar operating in a milieu of honesty, but also because he was exceptionally bright and had no shame. While we may wish the world were otherwise, it is a fact that the occasional pathological liar can be successful in any environment. This one was never "found out" and was promoted to the rank of rear admiral. Before he retired, in addition to wrecking his own family, he destroyed countless other professional lives.

In the main, however, institutions must be built on integrity. I spent a great deal of my life at sea. A warship in a rolling sea is chock full of opportunities for disaster. There are never enough experts to keep an eye on all the nooks and crannies. The Navy relies on trained human beings, the Navy terms them "watches," to monitor the equipment and spaces not covered by automatic sensors. Rising temperatures from any one single mechanical joint of the tens of thousands that exist needs to be noted immediately. Smoke or rising water levels call for immediate action. It isn't rocket science and the people who are assigned this work are often relatively junior and inexperienced. But the job does require an individual to stay awake and call for assistance when he finds something he doesn't understand. The lives of everyone on board are dependent upon the "watch" thinking and reporting abnormalities.

So the sea services insist on integrity. We drill on honesty. We insist on the absolute, unvarnished unforgiving truth. Every time. We require it in our training schools, on the engine room deck plates, and on the bridge. You only have to almost die once because someone fell asleep or failed to accurately report a high bearing temperature to develop a low tolerance for a "lack of integrity." If someone lies about what he or she did or didn't do, the first instinct of almost every sailor is to tell the miscreant to draw his or her pay and start walking.

Not only does integrity save lives, it conserves time, money, and intangibles. Once upon a time I was involved in the complex engineering evolution of overhauling a submarine. We had already been working at this task for more than two years at the cost of several hundred million dollars. We were months behind schedule. The job was harder than it had to be because the shipyard had made the strategic decision to abandon the nuclear power business and shift to the more profitable task of building gas-turbine-powered destroyers. The shipyard's conversion to its new business line was making our lives on the submarine difficult. Everyone in our crew was tired of working one-hundred-hour weeks as well as thirty-day months trying to assist the shipyard in keeping its submarine side of the shipyard above water while they raked in dollars on the surface ship side. Most of us had not had time off for a year. Our sailors were wearing down. And the delays the shipyard was causing in getting a submarine back to war against the Soviets were costing the American taxpayers a cool extra one million dollars each and every day.

One late evening we were set up to do a test that involved running the submarine's extensive hydraulic system. The goal was to pressurize and then inspect for leakage in the newly installed miles of welded high-pressure operating piping. We started the special pumps and BANG! Oil sprayed everywhere! One of the pipes had apparently failed. It seemed impossible given that each weld had been made by a qualified worker and inspected with the most advanced techniques. But oil was everywhere and there was a flared-out hole in the pipe. I had been observing the evolution and could have sworn I had seen out of the corner of my eye an unexpected quick and suspicious movement by one of our sailors. We immediately convened a critique.

I specifically asked the one individual who could have made an error that would have resulted in such damage (improperly closing and then immediately reopening a particular valve) if he had done what I suspected. He swore to me he didn't. I pressed him. He again denied it. I knew he was lying. While I was thinking about what to say next the commanding officer called me aside. The captain said he knew the man better than I did and he trusted the man's word. The captain knew I was not convinced. The captain volunteered that his own wife and the man's wife were close friends and the captain was also a teammate with the man on the local volunteer fire department. The captain said he trusted him. I was still unconvinced. The captain directed me not to question the man again.

It was decided that in the absence of definite proof, the shipyard would rip the entire ship's hydraulic system out and start over. This undertaking would mean an additional delay. It would require three weeks of around-the-clock effort and millions of dollars. Even more importantly, that rework introduced uncertainty in the crew's mind about everything the shipyard had done over the past two years. If ship-yard workers had made mistakes in the critical hydraulic piping, the piping that operated the few valves absolutely essential to submarine safety, where else might they have failed to do their best? Where might there be problems that might have not been adequately checked?

Since our submarine was going to be operating for months and years far below the surface of the sea, this uncertainty quickly bred fear. And as no one likes to acknowledge he is personally afraid, this fear was redirected and came to light as resentment toward the work-ers in the shipyard. It was especially expressed against those who had been responsible for welding the hydraulic piping into the ship. Within a day two fights between crew members and shipyard workers had broken out.

I was pretty sure at the time, and now know, that the individual I had glimpsed out of the corner of my eye had made a fairly basic mis-take. For you engineers, he had closed the discharge valve on a positive displacement pump, quickly realized his error, and then reopened it, but not quickly enough to prevent pipe-bursting pressures from devel-oping. But the man lied again and again until many years later at a submarine reunion, where he admitted the truth to me at the bar. But without that admission, which the captain did not let me press for at the time, none of us could be certain, and you don't take chances on the safety of a submarine that will carry people deep beneath the sea.

So, the Navy and the nation's taxpayers ate thirty million dollars more of overruns and our crew suffered another month of hundred-hour work weeks in a town where none of us wanted to be and where we were no longer welcome. Subsequently, three men in our crew of a little more than a hundred went absent without leave rather than face the perceived danger of going to sea in a ship "built carelessly" and, in those same tension-filled additional days, two more wives (of the thirty-four couples on board) filed for divorce.

Unlike a romance novel, there was no "happily ever after" to this story. The liar continued in his career for years longer, even after the captain was fired for a different error.

Integrity is always critical.

PART 3

Techniques a Leader May Find Useful

22 ★ LEADERSHIP APPROACHES

HOW DO YOU MEET *big* leadership challenges? What do you do when the organization has permitted the wrong personas to slither inside and curl up next to the fire? When racism and sexism or some other ugly-ism has taken up residence? When one or more of your leaders has lost his ethical compass?

I personally observed how a Chief of Naval Operations, specifically Adm. Elmo Zumwalt, tackled racism in the Navy. I used some of his same tactics in a later campaign I ran against sexism. Many people resented Zumwalt, but his campaign worked and made the Navy a much better place. So did mine.

In the early 1970s Admiral Zumwalt was facing a situation of overt racism. For two hundred years the Navy had been commanded and manned by white men. On board ship, minorities had historically been truly that. But the Navy was changing and was doing so in advance of America. Zumwalt had a practical professional reason for his actions. In order to maintain a sea service of the size America required, demographic experts predicted that the Navy ranks and ratings of the future would need to include black and Latino men, as well as women of all colors. The Navy had experienced technology changes before. They had been difficult. All change was. But the Navy had successfully changed from sail to coal and from coal to steam. Some even believed that the Navy was currently in the process of changing from oil to nuclear. The Navy knew how to prepare for and execute technology changes. But nothing was as difficult as culture change!

Admiral Zumwalt was personally prepared to proceed at full speed. But the Navy, like America, had deep-rooted problems that needed to be addressed. Near-daily riots on board ships confirmed this.

The magnitude of Zumwalt's challenge was not confined to the Navy. Congressional support for the Navy was historically anchored in the senators and representatives from the "Solid South." This Solid South was overrepresented on the four congressional defense committees: the Senate and House Armed Services Committees and House and Senate

Defense Appropriations Subcommittees. These were the men who provided the Navy its funding and direction. These were the men who had confirmed Zumwalt for his position and would vote on him again after two years if he hoped to get another term. They were essentially his Board of Directors, men who held the power of the purse for the Navy. In general, and certainly politically, they did not share Zumwalt's vision. Their collective political view might be best expressed as "wasn't it possible this race thing was being greatly exaggerated?"

Due to this divergence of congressional opinion, it was difficult for Zumwalt to use the normal leadership tools available to the Chief of Naval Operations. He could not fire racist Navy leaders and still keep congressional (and President Nixon's White House) support. He couldn't even quickly retire racist admirals. He could not rely upon the Navy "inspection" process to expose and correct racism on board ship. He instead was placed in the inconsistent position of conducting a public relations battle (for the audience inside the Beltway) to downplay the numerous race problems on board Navy ships while feverishly devising ways to change the culture within the Navy.

One of the methods he used was his "equal opportunity review." These reviews were conducted by minority Navy members from the various commands. The inspectors were fairly unobtrusive, as unobtrusive as minorities in a sea of practically all white sailors could be, and were intended to help the guy in charge lance any rising racial pressures. As might be expected, the Navy Old Guard reared up in real and imagined horror, especially those retired senior officers who purportedly remembered how things "used to be"! The latter complained about many things, including how any CNO could even dare to inquire about a leader's clearly racist statements or question unnecessarily putrid working conditions? Who ever listened to the dirt balls in a command anyway?

Then the Old Guard brought out their big guns, the charges that the review team members were all softies: chaplains and doctors. Some of them weren't even officers! The Old Guard got a great deal of press. Some in Congress loved them. Members of the House who weren't overly fond of Admiral Zumwalt's goals were particularly supportive.

This "equal opportunity" approach to combating racism, an unqualified strategic success when viewed from the perspective of a decade later, made Admiral Zumwalt very unpopular with his peers, many senior officers, and even junior officers of a certain mindset. From my perspective, the next CNO dumped most of Zumwalt's measures as quickly as he could think of a semirational reason. Fortunately, the "reviews" had already set the Navy on a new course that would greatly ease future race relations.

Years later, when I was in charge of about 10 percent of our Navy and the issue of the day was sexism, I put some of Zumwalt's lessons to use. I had become concerned that the senior leaders on one particular ship were taking actions that made Herman Wouk's infamous Captain Queeg look a bit namby-pamby. I understood that leaders needed the latitude to run their own organizations, but the tone of this organization was unnecessarily harsh. I wanted one particular commanding officer to understand that it would be better if he eased his approach (and that of his subordinates) to discipline. If he intended to continue his career, it would be best if he recognized his problem himself, and I wanted to give him another chance to do exactly that.

I mentally considered Admiral Zumwalt's "equal opportunity review" for a few days. I thought there might be a way to resurrect it. When the program was discarded, the press was briefed that the "review" had proven ineffective for small ships and commands. The great majority of Navy commands are relatively small. In small commands nearly everyone sees everyone else every day. The story the Navy had adopted was that small commands didn't need a bunch of do-gooders coming on board for two weeks and wasting everyone's time to deliver earth-shaking news like "Mr. Smith is a racist son of a bitch." Supposedly if you worked on board that ship, you already knew. Of course, although we clearly had our share, I never actually heard an officer identified as being either a racist or a son of a bitch. But no one in the media or elsewhere pursued the logical follow-up as to why we didn't reach down and fire these miscreants if we already could identify them. This particular logic was certainly not discussed in the press package that accompanied the semirational burial of the Zumwalt policies.

I knew how to make up my own story, and Zumwalt had been retired and gone for years. I built my own rationale around the difference between big and little ships. I gave the review a different name from the pariah title of Zumwalt days, informed my boss I was going to try an experiment, and promised to limit it to only a few large ships.

I also decided to experiment first on two of our best units to verify for myself that Zumwalt's system worked.

In selecting the review team, my staff proposed several different individuals. I quickly came to realize why the individuals selected for Admiral Zumwalt's review teams had seemed so milquetoast. We definitely were not interested in selecting a strong-willed individual who might inadvertently burn his or her personality into the command. We also weren't interested in having personal convictions inserted into the review's results. I also didn't want some meathead who couldn't listen to people and their problems. I wanted a fair judgment. Maybe I was dead wrong. Maybe the leadership team I wanted reviewed weren't jerks, but only irritated the hell out of me! In that case, I didn't want to leave scorched earth.

I needed individuals who projected an image of bland but bright. I wanted people who were patient, sincere, receptive, and interested in others. These are nice people to meet at a cocktail party but not necessarily the same sort of individuals who fill military leadership roles, so they weren't the ones I normally relied upon. But for this job I wasn't interested in a personality who would be inclined to grab a broken sword out of the sand, jump up, and swing over the wall crying "follow me!" I was casting a role for a man or woman who tended to sit under a tree on a park bench, the sleeves from a worn sweater draped around his or her neck, nodding pleasantly at the runners going by.

So we finalized a group and they sallied forth to spend two weeks on board a couple of our best commands, another week writing up their results, and then a month or two catching up on their day jobs. The first results matched our expectations. The team reported the crews were generally happy. The policies and procedures in use made sense to the inspection team as well as to the people on board the ship.

It wasn't all roses. The team found a couple of bad practices. I've forgotten the details. The commands, once informed, took appropriate action. We had not been dumb enough to tell the review team that we believed these were our two best ships for fear they would in turn simply reflect our own opinions, but the results were relatively consistent with what the previous staff inspections had shown. It looked to me like it was fine to proceed to the target ship.

Meanwhile, despite my best efforts to keep this whole event as low-key as possible, the commander of one of the two ships being reviewed had mentioned to his best and oldest friend in the Navy (who unfortunately was my boss) that we had inspected his command for a couple of weeks and not found much. In his rumination he had noted that he hadn't agreed with all the inspection results, and, since he wasn't running for elective office, he hadn't been too thrilled with polling being performed on board his command.

During my boss's next telephone call to me, he made it clear he thought these reviews had justifiably died with Admiral Zumwalt's retirement from the Navy (perhaps I had not fooled him terribly much about what I was doing), and this was an old idea he didn't wish to see resurrected. If we had the assets to do this sort of thing, we obviously had excessive staff!

It was a short phone call that I didn't overly enjoy.

Well, I could have followed his guidance, but then there would be no case study for you to read, would there? Instead, I decided to pick up the pace. I wouldn't know what I know now if I had followed his rather clear guidance, would I? I told the inspection team to immediately look at the next two ships, my target ship and another small ship that happened to be available. I had to throw in a small ship to get a second one since I had not planned to act so quickly and only one large ship was locally in port. The team was to follow the same process as before, spending two weeks on board each one getting to know the crew and then another five days writing up their report. But since I worried that my boss might cut the whole process short, after they had been on board a few days, I invited the inspection team leader to my office to give me a sense of both teams' progress. Wanting to distract him, I began by asking about the nontarget ship.

"Chaplain Dain (another fictionalized name), how are you finding things on board the USS _____?"

My guest was standing at attention as much as any chaplain can manage a military stance. "Not bad, Admiral. Certainly not as smooth as those first two ships, but not terrible. There are some complaints about privacy problems in the berthing areas. There are some sanitary conditions in the galley that need to be taken care of as soon as possible; the milk machine, in particular, leaks excessively and there are places underneath it that they don't . . ."

I closed my eyes for a second. I was hung up on his opening line, "not terrible." I interrupted him, motioning him toward a pair of oversized leather chairs. "Please sit down. Would you like coffee, chaplain?"

"No, sir."

I poured a cup for myself as my guest sat down. He began shuffling the notes in his lap, alternatively folding his hands and looking out the window at the rustling leaves on the large eucalyptus trees near the road as they stirred in the afternoon breeze. I watched him while I took a sip of coffee before I leaned forward, placed my arms across my legs, and stared directly at him. "Chaplain, what exactly would you classify as 'terrible'?"

The chaplain took a deep breath and looked down again at his notes. He moved one page to the back of his sheaf and silently read the now topmost sheet. I remained still, focused on him. He was about average height, sandy hair with sideburns that faded into his cheeks, maybe five pounds overweight, good-looking, a slight mustache neatly trimmed, completely nonthreatening. He had the perfect personality for relaxing people and learning their innermost thoughts. It was why we had selected him. It might be why he had originally become a chaplain.

Chaplain Dain was still looking at his notes. He raised one sheet that held a column of typed names, sort of half-offering it to me. "I think I would have said it was 'terrible' if the sex was nonconsensual, if the commanding officer had actually raped any of these eleven women." He finally looked directly at me, speaking more quickly as he did. "I realize even consensual sex with your crew members is against Navy regulations."

It certainly was!

His eyes dropped again to the sheet. "But none of these girls was under eighteen at the time. You know that is the age of statutory rape in California."

The chaplain now was staring at something in the distance over my right shoulder. "Of course, as a spiritual leader, since that particular commanding officer is married, I consider his behavior to be bad, but you specifically asked me to do this review in my capacity as a layman."

I was trying to mentally compose myself. It was against Navy regulations for an officer to have relations with any junior person in his command because of the authority he had over that person. It was also against regulations for a senior to have relations with a junior, for the same reason. It was also against regulations for a married person to have relations out of wedlock. I wasn't sure I could list all of the violations this commanding officer had committed, but even more egregious, he was a forty-year-old man using his position to take advantage of young people just starting out in life. It was also against Navy regulations for me to strangle a Navy chaplain in my office!

While I composed myself, I took a moment to consider the double-edged sword of selecting an unassertive review team. They had certainly been able to obtain information others had not; neither I nor any of my team had any clue this was going on. This was the small ship I had thrown in the mix at the last moment, *not* my target ship!

That afternoon, after I had arrested and replaced the commanding officer, I visited this ship and began speaking with the women on board. It turned out we had a horrible sexism problem on this ship, and we later found a similar issue on several other ships. We spent months working to make the situation better. I might never have known about the problem if we hadn't used nonthreatening people to identify an environment I and my team had been unable to sample.

Of course, timid people should not be expected to be the ones to understand what action is necessary or when and how to execute. They tend to be damn poor at it. That was my job.

By the way, I got so busy in working on fixing the sexism problem that I lost interest in making gradual improvements in the "target ship." Instead, one evening at a cocktail party I told the specific commanding officer he should quit being such a son of a bitch or I would fire him.

The military needs young people and those people may be different from the rest of America's workforce. That means the military must lead the country in social change. This inevitably creates tensions, for, while younger, the military population often retains America's regional and local chauvinisms. For the military leader, these bumps and lumps become opportunities.

23 ★ WELLINGTONS

NAPOLEON WAS DEFEATED AT WATERLOO, in present-day Belgium, by Field Marshal Arthur Wellesley, the First Duke of Wellington. There are probably several things you do not know about the good duke, including that he was Irish, not English, but the one I have always found most interesting is that he modified and wore the special boot named after him. The Wellington was originally a riding boot in which the leather shaft (the part that fits around the leg) rode high up on the wearer's ankle to deflect the weak musket balls fired from a distance. This higher shaft also protected the wearer's pants and ankles from the slop that is England (and Belgium) for at least one full season of the year. I have never particularly feared musket balls, but the boots have a blunt toe that I always have found particularly comfortable. The extra space permitted air to circulate around my toes in hot nuclear engine rooms. I am told that Wellingtons allowed room for the duke's feet to swell during long horse rides, known in some circles as equestrian journeys. Beats me. I know they worked well in nuclear submarines.

Floppy Wellingtons were the preferred wear for a young officer on a submarine who was lucky to catch even a couple of hours of sleep in any twenty-four-hour period. We expected at least one emergency wake-up every night, and frequently slept in our clothes. When the inevitable alarm horn sounded, I would slide fully dressed out of my bunk directly into my boots and be moving while the air disturbed by the alarm was still settling. I never wore any other shoes.

One day a group of inspectors came to evaluate our ship. The inspection process in the Navy tends to be cyclical. Sometimes it is the "in" thing. Then, after a few years, organizations decide they are being "looked at" so frequently they can't get anything done. Then inspections get dialed back. Most participants cheer at this point, for few believe they actually need inspections. And a review always results in more work and negative vibes.

Goodness knows, the rationale goes, people should be trusted; unnecessary inspections are a waste of time and some inspectors always get carried away with their own importance. No one ever seems to think that they may actually need some outside supervision, that it may not be second nature to everyone how to properly install, maintain, and run a three-story-high, double-ended, radially balanced, helix-wound, reciprocating turbotrasher.

During the period of this story, the inspection cycle was waxing, and regular and periodic engineering inspections were being introduced. Interestingly enough, these particular observers were not even regular naval officers, but civilians who had never even served in the Navy or on board submarines. Which made the attitude of those being inspected even more hostile. The inspectors had no idea of our problems! How could they do a valid job? Due to the luck of the draw, our ship was scheduled to receive one of the first of these inspections. Boy, were we excited!

Do you believe that?

Of course not. Well, we may have been excited, but it wasn't as in the sense of "glad." We were all good old Americans. As we would say to anyone who would listen (spouses, peers, dates, mothers, and barkeeps), "we are professionals with years of schooling and specialized training. We have survived the most difficult weeding-out process the Navy has and all of us are head-of-the-pack teams. Why in the world would we need an inspection?"

A few days before the planned date it became obvious the inspection would be even worse than we had expected. The faceless "they" were planning the very worst sort of review. This was not going to be a civilized inspection of whether we were keeping the double-ended, radially balanced whatchamacallit properly oiled and cleaned, or if the extensive files we had kept on that helix wound thingamajig were complete. Oh, no. It was going to involve all those things, as well as a written and oral examination of each of the operators, but a brand-new twist was included. These inspectors were planning to spend some time watching us do things. Normal evolutions. Routine evolutions.

Okay. Not a problem. Our enlisted personnel were well trained.

Inspection day dawned. I remember taking special care with my uniform. I wanted to be wearing one that was a bit faded to indicate I well understood the meaning of work but certainly one that didn't have an obvious hole, tear, or stain. I shaved carefully. I even polished my Wellingtons and shined my brass belt buckle. With butterflies in

my stomach, I reported with the rest of the officers to the wardroom
for assignment.

And then the inspectors arrived and announced that for this
inspection they would be asking *the officers* to conduct the evolutions
normally performed by the enlisted personnel. I was surprised, but
this was a submarine and every officer had performed every evolution
on board at least once. It was one of the mantras of submarining. We
also supervised hundreds of procedures every day. All of us were professionals. Not a problem.

A list of all the officers was posted beside the chromium-plated
wardroom coffee urn. The list paired us into two-man teams. Tasks
were to be assigned like square dance partners are chosen: by pulling
slips of paper out of a hat. The junior officer in each team would then
read the process for the procedure, with his partner operating the proper
valves, pumps, and switches. In our team I was to act as an assistant to
Roger, a much more experienced officer (and a made-up name).

Roger was the first officer to select a task. When he did, it was
quickly obvious we had drawn the easiest job by far. My partner was
one lucky son of a gun. Our job was surprisingly simple. We were to refill
a water expansion tank near the ceiling of one of the compartments of the
submarine. It was an easy task, one that, due to the design water leakage
that lubricated and cooled the mechanical and rotating elements in the
system, was necessarily performed three or four times each and every day.

Of course, there were some special considerations. The water we
were to use to fill the tank was a special grade, which because of possible trace radioactive contaminants was not, under any circumstances,
to be spilled. The fill water was kept under special conditions in a controlled location, and the expansion tank was indirectly connected with
the (truly contaminated) reactor systems, so the procedure wasn't quite
as simple as opening the valve on your garden hose. But our enlisted
people did this same evolution every day, and to be honest, neither
Roger nor I normally paid the slightest bit of attention to supervising
this particular task. How hard could this be? Both of us believed we
could do this in our sleep.

The details of this particular evolution are not especially important.
One simply opened a couple of valves to provide nitrogen pressure to
move the water along and then closed and opened a few other valves
to line up the water path, while carefully watching the sight-glass on

the side of the expansion tank to adjust the water to the proper level. Actually, there was one thing that required a bit of care. Because it was possible to put quite a bit of pressure on the sight-glass, it had been specially constructed. Consequently, you didn't actually see the water level, but rather observed a virtual level as the material conducted light differently when wetted on the inside. The light in the ceiling area of the expansion tank also wasn't especially bright. It consequently was iffy to discern the precise water level, especially while standing over near the water fill valve (that is, if you didn't use a partner to help you).

We each finished our coffee and Roger and I picked up our inspector, along with his ubiquitous clipboard. The three of us promptly moved off to get this portion of the inspection completed. Roger actually didn't think he needed my help. As we walked he made sure he told me this. As we reached the expansion tank I didn't even get the procedures book open before Roger began opening and closing valves. As quick as a wink, the familiar deafening roar of pressurized nitrogen rushing through the piping toward the water tank began reverberating throughout the small room. We could also hear water beginning to move in the piping, and both Roger and I looked up and concentrated on the sight-glass.

From where I was standing behind Roger the ceiling shadows made it difficult to see exactly how quickly the level in the sight-glass was rising. Out of the corner of my eye I saw Roger open the pressurizing valve a little more to increase the fill rate. The shriek of the air noise climbed even higher. I thought I could see the water level begin to ripple in the sight-glass. A few seconds went by. I couldn't see if the ripple was climbing any higher.

And then the water that was being improperly pushed to the overflow funnel slopped over the top of my Wellingtons, filling the insides of my newly polished boots all the way to my shins. I yelped with surprise (the water was cold!) and dismay! Roger and I looked down at the eight to ten inches of water in the room and then over at the inspector, who had climbed atop a pipe and was crouched well above the flood, furiously writing notes on the paper on his clipboard.

As you may guess, the memory of that inspection remains an embarrassment to me to this day.

We failed our inspection. It was traumatic. Our lives were miserable for several weeks as we worked long hours to fix our problems, starting first at the top with the officers failing to follow the procedures. While I remember that inspection as a single event, it was actually part of a process. Our submarine improved and passed the reinspection. The submarine force changed its training emphasis to include more attention to routine practices. The ships in which I later served were better as a consequence of my failure that day.

Whether the participants enjoy it or not, every organization needs "outside" reviews. Inspections don't violate special leadership or management concepts. But they do serve to provide otherwise unobtainable insight into the relative preparedness of an organization. Outside reviews thus serve as one of the key cogs in the gears of a continuous improvement program. In addition, just as the shocking current in a "sneak circuit" will get the attention of the electrician rewiring an old house, external inspections alert supervisors to particularly bad practices. They give you a chance to stamp out a small fire before it threatens to engulf the entire enterprise.

I have often wondered what would have happened if Roger and I both hadn't been wearing our Wellington half-boots? Certainly the water would never have risen so high and the lesson I learned would not have been so dramatic. I might not have so indelibly carried the memory of my soaked feet on to my next ship, where it quickly became clear that the problems were even worse!

My success there would lead me to wonderful career opportunities, and it all started when I was standing in a pair of wet boots. Which may be why I still favor Wellingtons today.

Institutions need reviews by outside organizations. If this doesn't happen, particularly in those "special" groups without natural competitors, it is easy to become complacent. Which is only a short step down the serene slippery slope to inadequate. That does not mean outside reviews are appreciated. They are generally accepted as cordially as the devil welcomes holy water. I never went through one, however, that did not generate some useful idea.

24 ★ LINE MANAGEMENT

DURING MY CHILDHOOD, my family escaped the brutal heat of Indiana summers by fleeing to my grandmother's Jersey home. There, the beach rose gently from the sea up to near her back porch screen door. Each retreating low tide left a manicured expanse of hundreds of feet of level packed sand, an inviting playing field. On this expanse children constructed forts and clamshell redoubts, while teens, when they awoke after tough nights walking the boardwalk, built miniature golf courses complete with roughs of slimy seaweed. As the adults dragged their chairs and umbrellas down to the sand, the clang of steel against steel from the horseshoe pits would begin as well as snippets of genteel conversations from the quoit and badminton courts. The in-between generations seized sticks from the flotsam along the high tide line to draw lines for early games of baseball, football, soccer, and volleyball.

Every daylight hour on the South Jersey beaches was filled with activity. But the king of beach sports was always handball!

For the noncognoscenti, beach handball is a marriage between tennis and ping-pong played without the net. An area the size of a volleyball court is carved on the hard sand. A small, soft, pink ("Philly") ball, slightly smaller than a baseball, is used, with human hands serving as paddles. The game requires quick reactions, rapid recoveries, and barefoot sliding stops on the drying sand. Hand-eye coordination is critical. Trash talking is optional but omnipresent.

I usually drew a court as soon as the tide retreated a bit more than halfway. It was a way of inciting my dad into a game. He had been nearly a world-class athlete and although his factory job and overtime hours made routine exercise impractical, he could never resist the lure of physical competition. Dad never wanted to lose. He was willing to keep the score close, but no matter how piercing my mother's stares from where she sat beneath her faded green-and-blue-striped umbrella, he could never bring himself to throw a game, even to one of his sons. I became more competitive as I got older, but our beach handball games were strictly no contest until I reached my middle teens and he was in his early forties. It was then that I first realized the importance of lines in the sand.

The closer I came to finally winning a game, the more I searched for ways to tip the scales in my favor! It was evident he had better hand-eye coordination, and I wasn't sure that would ever change. But I had lately noticed that Dad would sometimes tire and I was young; I could run forever. I surreptitiously began drawing the handball court a half or a full pace larger and hitting most of my early shots deep. I found I could get him to begin to gasp for air halfway through the second set. Eureka! The "brute force" of a larger court neutralized his skills!

As the summers went by, our roles reversed. It turned out his hand-eye coordination hadn't been genetically passed down, but then again, he never got younger. Now my mother was watching me closely to see if I was keeping the games close so both my dad and I could enjoy them. A smaller court rebalanced my advantage. I was the first person on the beach each day to covertly adjust the dimensions of our handball court based on the previous day's observations.

What did this beach game teach me?

A good leader is by definition thoughtful. Such leaders place their people in situations where they can succeed. Since each of your people has different skills, and the job demands constantly change, you need to be continually resizing your key players' courts. I certainly don't mean you shouldn't demand acceptable performance. If people cannot meet the organization's minimum standard, they need to be working some-where else. But if people are successfully performing above the estab-lished cut line, you will maximize the total output if you consider each individual—how they most easily take in information, how they emo-tionally work, and the product you want—*before* you sketch the specific lines in which you want them to operate. And you will reconsider those lines as the people grow and their personal situation changes.

The key is that no matter how your employees were originally selected, you have a cross-section of uncommon people working for you. Each has different skills, dissimilar kits in their toolboxes, and even disparate ways of absorbing information. Some may use reading or visualization, others need discussion, others will search for a way to manufacture a tactile memory in order to enhance understanding. In fact, scientists have found six different methods in addition to com-mon reading (auditory, verbal, physical, logical, social, solitary) that people use to study and retain information. Not only are people a dissimilar group in the way they learn, humans are emotionally different from each other. If you have a large enough organization, you have both introverts and extroverts and probably more personalities than Ms. Myers and her mother, Ms. Briggs, ever imagined.

It is important to appreciate where your employees fall on these different vert-graphs, or at least accept that there are differences, because their various personal skills and emotional temperaments should impact how you manage. Some of your men and women yearn to know precisely the product you desire, when you want it placed on your doorstep, and the color you prefer the decorative bow to be. These workers desire to see their manager daily and they need to routinely consult. If that doesn't happen, their work will be spotty at best. Many people, perhaps most people, appreciate the clearest and most complete guidance management can provide. Whether or not you yourself belong to that crowd, it is a sizable one and you need to provide the substance for which this group yearns.

This may well be the very style that propelled you to your professional success, but take care, for it also leads straight to two pitfalls. This same level of precision will drive some of your employees (often key ones) batty! Those individuals do not want team meetings or consultations. They want to be left alone with their impossible tasking. They despise group gropes and don't want compensatory time off. They only lust in their introverted hearts for more hours to work their own (logical, solitary) magic. Constraining everyone to only one problem-solving style inhibits individuals who have other dominant learning methods and personalities. If you force them all into one box they will vote their displeasure with their feet. The second danger is that solving problems differently is actually gainful! It tends to expose the criticality of key assumptions. These crosscurrents often lead to innovation, the lifeblood of any organization.

Back to that South Jersey beach.

One of the most difficult tasks of a leader is keeping everyone working the issues of the day, while concurrently staying alert to the ideas/concepts/technologies that will be the growth engines for tomorrow. Revolutions in military affairs are made possible when you take a stick from the high-tide-line flotsam and chalk individual lines for each of your remarkable people.

Just as I discovered during those long ago summers, good "line" management produces a better game.

A team performs best when you recognize the individuality of the members. Each person solves problems differently. Marv Langston, the first CIO of the Pentagon, tried to emphasize this by having everyone add their particular Myers-Briggs four classification letters to their name tags. The question is always: How may I best take advantage of these varied skills in my organization? This can usually be done by making a few minor changes in the job roles. Often no one even notices if one or more of the common boundary lines has bulged out or sucked in a bit. If any complaints are made, they are assumed to be from the usual carpers, they are ignored, and you still will have a better organization.

25 ★ PROCESS IS INSUFFICIENT

OUR MILITARY POWER IS SUSTAINED by our economic power. Our more influential citizens are therefore often those who made it possible for the United States to establish our dominant capitalistic position. In my personal hall of fame, I have a wall reserved for three men who were instrumental in ensuring that American democracy stands atop the world.

My first portrait is of the man who actualized the integrated circuit revolution, the man who originated the Six Sigma processes: Bill Smith from Motorola. As you may know, the impetus for Bill's work was the early need generated by those companies trying to put together products with the fancy new integrated circuits that everyone was inventing in the 1970s. These were the early complex calculators, computers, etc., being manufactured by companies like Motorola and Texas Instruments.

There were many chips in these products, in some cases thousands or tens of thousands. With the wiring of these in series and the common chip reliability of the day, and a failure rate of 1 percent or perhaps as low as a tenth of a percent, the inevitability of mathematics produced high product failure rates. Early product deaths meant terrible word-of-mouth results, even before social media, and consequential low sales. The products themselves might be fast and flashy, but people simply were not willing to put up their hard-earned dollars for something that might suddenly go silent!

This all changed when Bill Smith helped Bob Galvin, the CEO of Motorola, prove that Motorola could achieve extraordinary higher component reliabilities by changing human (Motorola worker) habits. He promised to make radical improvements without expensive new machines. Galvin wanted a 10 to 15 percent improvement in Motorola revenue. Bill more than delivered. And he then taught his techniques to those interested. American industry surged forward.

My second picture is of W. Edwards Deming, the famous Plan-Do-Check-Act man. Dr. Deming insisted on establishing and maintaining exacting standards—some that had never before been achieved—in manufacturing. Once established, these new criteria were so precise that a component constructed by one production line could actually be interchanged with a similar part made in another machine shop. Standards that are common today, but unheard of at that time. Before Deming, a series of valves, although reportedly identical, were actually so different from each other that a valve made to fit on the port side of a ship might not work when placed in the same relative position on the starboard side of the same ship. I had this happen to me at least once.

Deming's practices not only revolutionized manufacturing, they also revolutionized logistics. Dr. Deming's principles were so successful that he was seen as instrumental in reestablishing the Japanese manufacturing economy after World War II. After that monumental achievement, Dr. Deming returned home in time to save Ford from bankruptcy against the powerful competition Deming himself had built at Toyota and Honda.

The third portrait on my mental wall is that of Hyman G. Rickover. Rickover not only built the first operating nuclear reactor in the world and supervised the construction of America's most powerful nuclear submarine fleet, he also drove the establishment of a new industrial base in America. It was built to the exacting standards necessary to support working with nuclear energy. It was a new technical field that emphasized precision, exactness, and repeatability. He essentially insisted that everyone adopt both Smith's and Deming's practices. Rickover also added a caveat for nuclear power. Rickover insisted that no one, no matter how tired or sick, could make even one error. He frequently reminded everyone, military and civilian, of one simple homily: "You never go home at night to the wrong house. Then why would you make a mistake on my reactor?" The nuclear submarine fleet he built was a major factor in the success of the Cold War against the Soviet Union. To this day, U.S. nuclear submarines continue to operate worldwide without ever experiencing a reactor accident.

These three men have had an impact on nearly every management book written in the past fifty years. Which certainly doesn't mean that they have aided the general confusion about the differences between leadership and management. People use these two general words to refer to a wide spectrum of issues. Smith and Deming weren't worrying about risk. They were addressing manufacturing problems. They

Adm. Hyman G. Rickover. The father of the Nuclear Submarine Force. An unstoppable force. The man who provided our presidents the tools to win the Cold War. *Naval History & Heritage Command*

developed tools for that specific purpose. Their tools can be stretched to work in other circumstances—sometimes—as long as everyone takes the time to understand his or her limitations. More often, trying to adapt management tools to leadership problems is largely a waste of everyone's time.

And, whatever your organization, you need high standards. Standards are the basics. And if you have standards, you need processes to maintain those standards. Those are the two givens.

After that it gets harder to stretch process lessons to cover leadership. Take care. You don't want to go down the wrong path. Standards and processes are surprisingly easy to unwittingly abuse. If well-intentioned people ratchet a particular standard tighter without balancing costs, the process's purpose, and the integrated mission, the organization will soon find it is wasting time and money. Attention can be diverted away from what is important. In the Navy nuclear power program, early on we lost control of some of the humans who had their hands on the ratchets. We let our organization be driven by a few individuals' idiosyncrasies instead of organizational goals. It took an enormous effort for the nuclear power program to unscrew itself and get reoriented. At the same time, if a process has been unchanged for a decade, it should receive careful review. Is it even possible that something can pass unscathed through three technical half-lives and a human generation?

Everyone needs periodic reinvention to keep from going out of business. While important, standards and processes are merely the pots and pans in the kitchen of the organization. The quality and preparation of the food, the ambiance, and the service are what make the restaurant a success. Similarly, the real question for any business is how to get the team to pull together and deliver the X percent improvement each quarter (where X depends on the product line) necessary to improve market share or profit margin. And when the team is successfully doing this, you can then face your real challenge.

How do you get the same people who are delivering day-to-day results to also think out of the box? Businesses constantly need to be redeveloped. Someone is always thinking of a better way, a less expensive way, to get even better results—to achieve—or to be something that the public didn't even realize it wanted. That someone has to be your team. Every organization faces this problem. I find it seldom works to have special groups or consultants doing your thinking for you; they don't understand the interrelationships of your business as well as your own people do. But a "quality circle" recommendation often doesn't quite get you to the level of a survival breakthrough. So you may need a stranger to kick-start discussions or to introduce your own rule-breaking ideas.

There are as many ways to present change as there are leaders. Not every leader sees a need for subterfuge or the requirement to develop consensus. In the thirty years Admiral Rickover held significant sway over the nuclear submarine force, he made several decisions that altered the basic design and operation of nuclear submarines. Each was made against the collective advice of his staff. All were heavily criticized. Historically, each proved critical to the triumph of American nuclear submarines.

One of the early key decisions the admiral made in the late 1940s had to do with the reactor shielding for nuclear submarines. Rickover decided American submarines would be designed to expose sailors to a radiation level less than 1 percent of the level world experts had told him was safe. Since neutron and gamma shielding is bulky and heavy, there were immediate real-world consequences. The most obvious one was that American submarines would be slower than their Russian counterparts.

This was not a popular decision in the Navy, on Capitol Hill, or anywhere. Speed is life in combat. Admiral Rickover's technical director, Ted Rockwell, the man who actually wrote the book that is still used today on reactor shielding, was one of many who told Rickover he was being too conservative. Ted told me that Admiral Rickover ignored him, as well as everyone else, on this subject.

This initial speed design disadvantage remained with American submarines forever. It drove the United States to make significant investments in quieting and sonar processing. If the relative advantage of speed were lost, then Americans would have to achieve dominance in the other components of the kill chain. As it turned out, these were exceptionally fortunate choices. Computer processing advances powered exponential improvements in quieting and sonar processing while, despite many different efforts, speed could only be linearly adjusted upward by brute power. At the same time, the high radiation level due to lower shielding on board Russian submarines had a deleterious effect on their sailors. The Russians soon developed blood cancers that required time away from their submarines to recover. This prevented any Russian officer from having nearly the same time at sea as his or her American counterpart. Over the years of the Cold War the cumulative effects of these differences became evident in their professional performance. We won.

Another abrupt change of direction by Rickover was equally startling and difficult to implement. The first nuclear submarine was commissioned in 1954, the second in 1956. In 1969 the majority of attack submarines in the Navy were still diesel-powered, yet Admiral Rickover made the decision, again against the advice of his staff, not to permit radioactive liquid to be released from ships in port.

This unilateral decision caused great anguish in the submarine force. The ships were a pressurized water reactor design. Admiral Rickover himself had insisted on that particular design. As every science fair student knows, water expands and contracts with temperature changes. To conduct necessary repairs and save money, the submarines frequently cooled down as soon as they entered port. That meant they had to heat up and expand before they left again. But early submarines were not designed with internal holding tanks for any radioactive wastewater. Thus, up until the day the admiral made his decision, small quantities of radioactive isotopes had been diluted and permitted to be sent over the side on outgoing tides. The piers and general areas in which discharges were made were then monitored, and detailed records were kept.

I remember the day Rickover made his decision on radioactive discharges. I was in New London, Connecticut. I was the engineer officer on the USS *Nautilus* (SSN 571), the first, and thus the oldest, nuclear submarine. It was around noon when we heard of the new policy. I remember because my commanding officer was at Rotary giving a speech about why our nuclear discharge policy (the one that had been okay yesterday) was so safe to the environment. Unlike some of the newer submarines, my ship's design specifically planned for the primary plant to be cooled down when in port! Consequently, we were "cold." I was planning to start up later that afternoon to get under way. To do that I needed to heat up the plant several hundreds of degrees. I needed to dump a whole bunch of water somewhere. Obviously, after Admiral Rickover's announcement, no longer was any water going to splash into the Thames River! I needed to find a new solution.

With this decision on radioactive discharges, Rickover once again demonstrated his ability to see over the horizon. What was there lying in wait? After some early protests against nuclear weapon testing in the late 1960s, Greenpeace would be founded in 1971. By the time it got around to focusing on nuclear submarines, the potential Achilles heel of radioactive isotopes damaging the environment had nearly decayed away to disappear below background levels. The Navy's problems with Greenpeace and its supporters were appropriately limited. If we had not stopped dumping water overboard, however, it would not have mattered how good and detailed our processes were. We would have been hammered by the new emphasis on environmentalism. The United States military might well have been severely harmed at precisely the wrong time in the Cold War.

The real title of this chapter should be "Process Is Insufficient, Leadership Is Essential." Process and standards make the work easier in all organizations. If you don't have processes, they are worth establishing. Once in place, there are some concerns I have outlined, but the real work continues to be about the mission of the organization, whether it is providing services to the public or making money. That requires management to meet the immediate and long-term goals and leadership to be focused on ensuring the organization grows at the desirable rates or adapts to changing circumstances.

As an example of why process is never enough, let us return to the pictures on my wall. After thirty years of working at his own institute establishing his Six Sigma tool, Bill Smith, my first hall-of-fame picture, instituted that powerful tool at Motorola in 1987, a too-big-to-fail company by any measure. In 1988 Motorola would consequently be awarded the very first prestigious Malcolm Baldrige National Quality Award (MBNQA) and gather record profits. Bill died of a heart attack at work in the Motorola cafeteria in 1993.

Bob Galvin, the brilliant chairman and CEO who grew Motorola and hired Bill, fully retired in 1999. His son, Chris, became the chairman and CEO and announced a new dedication to Six Sigma. But Chris was not his dad. After billions of dollars in losses associated with a satellite communications venture (Iridium) that he approved, Chris was pushed out of the company after four terrible years. In 2002 Motorola again won the Baldrige award. They were one of only seven repeat winners ever! And, as of 2019, there have been only 123 awardees. It was, however, an exceptionally hollow and misguided gesture. Only nine years later Motorola would be declared defunct as a business. Half of the remaining company would be sold to the Chinese.

Process is always insufficient; leadership is essential.

26 ★ ALIGNMENT

NEW IDEAS ARE THE PRICELESS diamonds of any organization. But as inevitably as clouds foretell rain, new discoveries bring change, and change makes people uncomfortable. How then does one convince skeptics that ugly rocks with a pit of sparkle are worth cutting and polishing? One way is to force the skeptics to also assume the role of the prospectors. Make them glimpse the first sparkle. Let me give you a case study.

In December of 1989, on the Soviet cruise liner *Maxim Gorky*, off Malta, President George H. W. Bush met with soon-to-be president Gorbachev of the Soviet Union for conversations that essentially ended the Cold War. The Navy Pentagon staff, who were perhaps closer to the true significance of this event than the other services because of the intelligence role nuclear submarines had played in the Cold War, recognized the importance of this meeting and began appropriate long-term planning.

I had been assigned as the Navy's planning officer for my first flag officer assignment. With this perspective behind me and another two years spent commanding the attack submarines on the West Coast, I was sent back to the Pentagon to head a large staff responsible for pulling together the entire naval budget for the Secretary of the Navy and the Chief of Naval Operations. To facilitate this work, I was double-hatted to both the Chief of Naval Operations and the Secretary of the Navy. To give me the power to set some agendas, I was titularly the senior two-star in the Navy. I arrived at the Pentagon shortly after the historic meeting on board the *Gorky.*

What had Malta meant for the Navy? We needed to decide. I began by scheduling meetings of the Washington-area two-star Navy admirals and Marine generals twice a week at 5 a.m. Why such an hour? The Navy is a polite place and we don't say things about people behind their backs. Thus admirals who don't desire to defend their programs simply only need to find a reason they can't attend a meeting and rely on courtesy to keep anything from happening. It is difficult for anyone to find a scheduling conflict at 5:30 in the morning. In 1990 most of the admirals and generals running the Navy and Marine Corps were just happy that the Cold War was over. They didn't see that a money crunch was inevitable or any need to reexamine our naval focus. On the other hand, a few of us believed we were in a race against time.

I wanted this group of thirty or forty officers to have the opportunity to review the entire Navy and Marine Corps. I understood that my fellow flags might never be able to break years of established culture and publicly ask critical questions of their peers. I was willing to take the point but I wanted everyone to hear my questions and hear the answers, or the nonanswers.

There was an underlying belief at that time (certainly not an agreement, but an understanding) that some programs, such as nuclear power, personnel, and aviation, were sacrosanct. I wanted every component of the Navy to hear the sacred cows being carefully prodded, if not roasted. My staff and I could provide enough heat to make it evident to everyone that each area had been examined. I needed my peers to hear the responding staffs try, in public, to defend their own cows and programs. I also wanted, in everyone's presence, to turn over all the apple carts. Either rats ran out in front of us all or it would be found to be a well-packaged assortment. Everyone could then make their own decisions and we could all help reload.

The Navy and Marine Corps was a nearly hundred-billion-dollar organization held together by a number of relationships and perhaps a few secret handshakes. If we were going to change it—and who but we were better prepared to lead that change—then we should understand the organization as best we could. I believed that this was the only way we could build any sort of consensus. For this to work, however, all the key flags and general officers were going to have to be physically together during an extended review. I was fairly sure I could gain everyone's interest the first time I publicly attacked one of the sacred cows, but that would be a high-wire effort, and I wasn't willing to take that risk for less than a full house. All the flags and generals had to be paying attention the first time. This wasn't something for them to hear secondhand.

To make the group exclusive, I specified that only the invitee could attend (i.e., he couldn't send another admiral or general as a replacement without my permission). To add suspense, a written schedule was published of areas my staff planned to brief. We didn't plan for any area to escape review. To begin that process, I brought in three civilians who were immune from pressure from leaders of the Navy and were then among the most respected futurists in the United States: Jack Gansler, who headed a commercial analysis organization and would later become undersecretary of defense for acquisition for President Clinton; Dov Zakheim, CEO of the analytical firm System Planning Corporation who would become the Pentagon comptroller for President George W. Bush; and Phil Odeen, who was then the managing partner of the accounting firm Coopers & Lybrand. I also gave contracts to two federally funded research and development centers: the Institute for Defense Analysis (IDA) and the Center for Naval Analyses (CNA). We asked each of them the same questions about the future. Then I had my staff pull on loose threads.

After two years of some heated early-morning discussions, we had developed a rough conviction, if not a consensus. Our conclusion was that no peer competitor to the United States would arise for a couple of decades and we could safely adjust our investments in stealth airplanes and submarines in order to increase our capability in littoral combat.

This concept may have been based on good analysis, but for the Navy it was truly a radical departure from the past. I can't pretend we had consensus. In many quarters there was only grudging acceptance. Many of us had been fighting the Soviet Union our entire careers. For that period the military budgets had advocated only the most capable platforms, and now we were considering advocating the termination of some of the air and subsurface platforms that had been the reflections of thirty years of Cold War thinking. There had been a good reason for that approach. The Soviet Union had presented a capable threat and we had been in an arms race. Now the Navy was proposing to deliberately choose to underbuild in the two areas (air and submarine) where we had a proven technical advantage over the Soviets!

Even though the meetings had been held before the sun came up, a number of key admirals and generals had seen a glint!

One of a leader's most important tasks is to plan how change will be achieved. In this one, we evaluated how the entire Navy and Marine Corps should adapt to the post–Cold War environment. We had briefings on different subjects (some repeated) twice a week for two years. We wouldn't have reached consensus if we had talked for a century. But we built a rough conviction.

Some gigs are bigger than others, but leadership is leadership.

27 ★ WHAT ARE YOU WILLING TO PAY?

SOMETIMES, THE SOLUTION IS simply finding the penalty you are willing to pay.

In the early 1980s I was sent to take over the team of men and women directing submarine operations in the Pacific against the Soviet Union. This particular job had destroyed several careers. Not only was it tactically challenging, it was a politically difficult role in which the holder, with a several-hundred-person staff in Yokosuka, Japan, managed all the Allied submarines against the Soviet Union as well as the other challenges in the China and Asia area. This charge was difficult, but the icing on the cake was that the job's personal reporting chain branched off to three different admirals, each of whom had dramatically different responsibilities. With different responsibilities come disparate evaluations of the priorities, and goodness knows there are never sufficient assets.

Three different reporting chains was a situation that begged for trouble. In addition, for reasons I will enumerate, the 1980s were a time of great tension between the submarine force and the rest of the Navy. Yokosuka had thus become a battlefield for the Navy's divas. After several careers had been charred, a particularly wise man, Rear Adm. Bud Kauderer, had sent me there to "get things back on track." I knew I had to deal with misunderstandings first.

Nuclear submarines had never been well understood in the Navy. After the Soviet spies embedded in British intelligence in the 1950s (Don Maclean, Guy Burgess, and Kim Philby) took the Polaris 616–class submarine plans to the Soviet Union (from which the Soviets developed their own fleet known forever after as the Yankee Class), Admiral Rickover spearheaded a deliberate effort to keep even the most mundane submarine details cloaked in secrecy from everyone, even the rest of our own Navy. This had been ironclad. Even my wife had never been in the nuclear engineering spaces. She had no "need to know" even though she had a Top Secret security clearance because of her job as the undersecretary of the Navy's counsel!

In addition, submariners were becoming increasingly reluctant to pay obeisance to the carrier, the centerpiece of normal Navy operations. That was primarily because of safety concerns. Submarines didn't work well within the carrier screen protection concepts of the time. Submarines aren't like other surface ships. Subs are clumsy on the surface and don't operate well near other ships. Submarines are bloody difficult to communicate with and not only don't have good radars of their own, they don't give off a decent radar reflection. By comparison, at any moment, surface ships have a dozen circuits to communicate on, have more radars than Zeus has lightning bolts, and reflect rays like a big tin barn in a Kansas wheat field. This meant that gathering around the carrier, which was the accepted formation of the day, was an open invitation for a submarine to bump into something or for that something to plow over a submarine.

Given that real danger, just as aviators insisted on having someone who had earned wings on their chest be involved in telling pilots when and where to fly, submariners wanted only someone who had earned the right to wear dolphins to be involved in having the final say about where and how to drive submarines. They also wanted to start this process by having the submarines far, far away from the carrier.

Submariners were sometimes loath to actually acknowledge that weaknesses in the communication and maneuverability of their platforms led them to need these safety measures. There were also several more reasons for the various branches to develop a good "mad on." At the time, submariners and aviators were both paid more than surface officers. The aviators weren't sure the submariners deserved the same pay the aviators were receiving because none of the "bubbleheads" were dying in Vietnam. In perhaps petty retaliation, the 50 percent of officer aviators in the Navy successfully changed the rules to drastically limit personal valor awards to submariners. Only the submariners, however, were carrying the top secret war against the Soviet Union, and when it came to who best deserved to wear those little bits of colored ribbons, nuclear submariners hadn't noticed a lot of aviators inside the *Thresher* or the *Scorpion* as these boats spiraled to the bottom of the ocean. Meanwhile, diesel submariners weren't sure they were fond of anyone in the Navy.

Meanwhile, back within the Washington Beltway, Admiral Rickover had rejected several officers for service on submarines who still subsequently made flag (and Admiral Zumwalt had publicly rejected Rickover and become CNO). These men sometimes encouraged friction. And, of course, even in the same service some people just don't like each other. All these years of nicks and nits built up a good supply of dry tinder that was just waiting for any spark such as an ill-considered phrase in a senior official's speech. If social media had existed at the time, I can't imagine how any of us would have survived!

I decided I would overcome the safety and security misunderstandings by a blitz of information. I surmised that if I were willing to travel tens of thousands of miles monthly to continually assure the half dozen admirals in the far Pacific that I had their best interests at heart, explain face-to-face what our submarines were doing for them, address specific questions they had, and move submarines as much as possible to be responsive to their needs, I might move the needle of their concerns. I wouldn't budge on submarine safety principles, but I could talk, talk, talk. I requested and got two more deputies assigned. We three worked side-by-side for sixty days and I left the operating business to them and was off into the air to begin my cajoling tour. For several months I was in airplanes many more hours than I was on land or on water. Slowly, personal diplomacy and professional flexibility began to carry the day.

Of course, life is not simple, and while things were getting better with my peers and the two nonsubmarine flags I was reporting to, the submarine admiral who had ordered me to my job rotated out and I soon became aware of a festering problem back at my old command. There was always a dearth of experienced senior submariners. The officer I had relieved in Yokosuka (one of the ones who had previously been "charred") had been assigned to Oahu as head of operations for submarines in the Pacific. He was only responsible for the submarines operating near Pearl Harbor, but he knew that the most exciting operations were those being conducted in our region. Those are the operations he most wanted to brief his boss on, and, honestly, he knew a lot about what we were doing. Perhaps, being only human, he may have been a little jealous of the generally positive reports now beginning to roll in on my performance. I wouldn't have been surprised if the tone of his briefings about our operations had begun to take on a note of uncertainty, like, "We're not sure what Dave's doing with *Guardfish*

Vice Adm. Bud Kauderer. His exceptional judgment made him trusted by everyone. *U.S. Naval Institute photo archive*

down in Thailand, we know the queen wants her daughters extracted so they aren't threatened by the mob closing on Pattaya. The president promised we would do this, but we haven't seen any traffic yet and Dave hasn't called me back; he may be off on another one of those social visits to the carrier he seems to think so important."

That night, as the queen's daughters departed in a submarine, I stood on the pier at Pattaya Beach looking at a dispatch from one of my Hawaiian friends and giving it some thought. I could launch a backfire effort in Oahu, but I was always going to be busy four thousand miles away and my problem would be at headquarters each and every day. I could not fix his hurt feelings, and I was never going to operate the submarines the same way he had. My predecessor had seldom disrupted submarine schedules. I frequently did so. I was not going to alter that pattern. I believed it was a reasonable price for the submarine force to pay to show the aviators and surface officers that those submarines not currently engaged with the Soviets were willing to do their best to help train the American fleet.

The real problem was that those changes were making my predecessor look bad. Every time he told his admiral (and one of my three bosses) what a submarine was doing, the admiral would find out later in the day the submarine was doing something different! This was all driven by the five-hour time difference between Hawaii and Japan. All Navy commands do early morning operational briefings. When my predecessor's staff was preparing to brief his boss on what my submarines were doing that day, my key people were asleep. Consequently my predecessor was frequently being embarrassed, for before they had gone to bed my senior operators had often tasked our submarines with doing something new. Those changes would then become evident in Hawaii only after the morning Oahu briefing. Resentment was continuing to build.

I wasn't willing to change what we were doing differently; I believed my new policies were reducing tensions between us and the aviators and surface officers. But after several weeks of worsening relations between the two submarine staffs, I finally asked myself the right questions: If I weren't going to reverse my course of action, was there a price I was willing to pay to make our internal submarine problem go away? If I were willing to literally spend two weeks each month in an airplane to solve problems with my peers, what price was I willing to pay to make peace with someone who should be a friend?

Thought of this way, the answer was simple. If, late each night, a couple of people sat down and evaluated what we had considered and where we were sending everyone and made only one copy of that information—and had it sent by a special circuit to an envelope that was placed smack in the middle of my predecessor's desk shortly before he was to brief the big cheese in Oahu—he was again the authority! Now my predecessor was again the only person in the Hawaiian headquarters who knew where all my submarines were and what they were doing and why. His status was re-established. It just cost a few of us some sleep.

After a week or so, we made a telephone call and a not-so-subtle threat. If he continued to support our new flexible efforts, we would also continue to make the extraordinary effort required to give him all the fascinating information. If not, we would probably be a little late in delivering information. Still within standards, of course, but unfortunately too late for his morning brief.

Life got easier. I had bowed my head and found a penalty I was willing to pay. That is often the situation with a leadership problem: You simply have to decide what the objective is worth and pay the piper. Pride often makes leadership unnecessarily harder.

28 ★ RISK REQUIRED

A LEADER FREQUENTLY NEEDS SPECIALISTS. These are those men and women with completely different training and expertise such as lawyers and doctors. Their advice can fill gaps in knowledge and reduce decision risks. At the same time, their counsel, no matter how expert, should never be permitted to take the place of leadership.

I once took over an organization that was rumored to be a veritable den of sexual harassment problems. In the year before I arrived, about six or more women had made assault accusations. Each investigation had produced inconclusive results. Rather than do something constructive to address the "environment," the leadership had transferred the women to less responsible roles in the organization. I had seen this before. In my experience, lawyers may sometimes not be the best investigators; they spend too much time looking for sufficient facts and too little time listening to their guts. A half dozen cases of alleged sexual assault is not just smoke, it is a roaring bonfire!

Since the problem has changed too damn little in the fifty years since Zumwalt introduced women into the main military branches, let me summarize it. There are still too many people who personally believe that if women ever achieve a position as professionals equal to men in the military, unbridled sex in the workplace is inevitable, thus threatening good order and discipline as well as religious chastity and marital vows. As someone who has been present throughout this transition, this grossly misrepresents the situation. The watercooler scuttlebutt always was that married men who had been so inclined had always managed to have a whole hell of a lot of sex when the military was an all-male body. Thus, the introduction of women into the military, rather than encouraging sex in the workplace, instead has had the effect of humanizing the military. The men who were true remain that way and the existence of professional women peers has improved men's respect for women. That there is still too much bad sexual behavior is only an indicator of the extraordinary amount of inappropriate conduct that occurred in the past.

To return to the scene of an earlier case study, one day in sunny San Diego my command received an anonymous telephone call alleging that one of my married, forty-year-old logistic supervisors was having sexual relations with his twenty-something secretary. The attorneys began an investigation. The supervisor and the secretary both denied everything and no one could be found who would testify they had actually witnessed the two engaged in public displays of affection. There were certainly no correlating Mr.-and-Mrs.-Smith motel records in the vicinity of Ballast Point.

On the other hand, the investigation uncovered some potentially interesting facts, including that the enlisted woman with duties as a secretary seemed to always get more time off than the other secretaries, frequently engaged in closed-door conferences with her boss, and had gone on weekend boat trips with both her supervisor and his wife. In addition, the secretary had told several of her non-Navy girlfriends that she had engaged in sex with her boss. Unfortunately, the investigators believed she had been too vague for them to establish independent corroborating evidence, and all of her civilian "friends" were reluctant to appear in any court. All her military coworkers, however, were more than eager to testify that the secretary changed her clothing (civilian to a uniform or vice versa) in her boss's office at the beginning and end of each day, even when he was present. The investigator reported that the secretary was much smarter and probably more mature than her supervisor. The investigator opined to me that he believed she knew exactly what she was trading for extra benefits.

My attorney advised me to let a prosecutor sort out the facts and let a court establish justice and any appropriate penalties. She said that if I were to do anything other than recommend a court-martial, given my seniority, the parties would be able to later claim the court and jury had been "unduly influenced."

I had no reason to believe she wasn't legally correct. At the same time, I had only been in my job for a couple of months and I was already beginning to see a pattern as to how the senior officers in my command treated women. There was this case, in which the secretary's behavior was basically undermining all the other Navy women who needed to make a living and weren't interested in trading sex for favors (although men seemed to think they were). There was a second case, in which a woman had come to me to say that a year earlier she had tried to report circumstances of sexual assault, but had been ignored and transferred to less desirable responsibilities. Later her assailant was promoted. The woman maintained that hers was not the only harassment case the organization had not taken seriously. And I had just received a report of a married man having consensual relations with more than a dozen young women in his organization. I wanted an immediate attitude readjustment across the command. I needed the red glare and boom of a rocket bursting in the sky overhead to illuminate what was new and different in Dodge.

I had about six or seven hundred midlevel or more senior supervisors working for me and an auditorium that would hold all of them. I asked my staff to gather these individuals. I gave two days' notice so everyone could be present. While time ticked by, I had my chief of staff make some private arrangements.

That day marked the first general address I had made since I took command. I took some care with the staging. I even cribbed a bit from what I remembered from presidential State of the Union addresses, with my chief of staff and the staff attorney standing behind me on the podium. I kept my remarks relatively brief. I confined them to the importance of our job of keeping nuclear submarines at sea against the Soviet threat and my concern about three specific items: alcohol abuse, suicide prevention, and the importance of women to our Navy. I only spoke for ten to fifteen minutes. I didn't want anyone to fall asleep. The woman issue was last, and I let everyone know it was personal to me. Finally, it was time for the big finish. "Lieutenant Commander Peters (again, a fictionalized name)," I said. "Stand up." I heard a gasp from behind me. I recognized my attorney's voice.

I pointed to a man in the audience. "Yes, Mr. Peters, that's you. Stand up." He stood and everyone turned and partially rose in their seats as necessary to get a look at the person I was speaking to. He was a slight man with a wispy mustache and early pattern baldness. Behind me I sensed that my attorney was resisting reaching forward to grasp my arm. I could see the two large sailors I had asked for stepping out from either side of the auditorium and wading into the audience toward Mr. Peters.

"Ladies and gentlemen, Lieutenant Commander Peters doesn't care about the rules that have previously been established by the Navy or our society. Although he is married he has been having illegal sex with a young enlisted yeoman that works in his office." Again, that inadvertent gasp from behind me. The two men had reached Lieutenant Commander Peters. I paused to let them get the handcuffs on him. Now his chair was being folded and set aside and one man was kneeling down to install metal shackles and short chains around his shins. The people around him were now all standing, and Peters was beginning to shuffle between his guards toward the door. People in the row in which he had been sitting folded or pulled their metal chairs aside as Mr. Peters was accompanied out of the auditorium to the paddy wagon outside the auditorium door.

I made my final statement from the podium. "He is being escorted to jail. You won't see Lieutenant Commander Peters in a Navy uniform again."

I turned to walk off, leaving my chief of staff to inform the group that I was sponsoring a barbecue in a field behind the gymnasium and they were all welcome to attend, nearly stopping when I saw my lawyer. There were tiny rivulets of bright red blood running down from both her nostrils to her upper lip. She feared I had just screwed up the legal case. I suspected she was absolutely correct and that both Lieutenant Commander Peters and his secretary (who also had been simultaneously arrested that day) would eventually walk on their charges. Many months later they did, and a judge admonished me from the bench. But by the time the legal system would reach its eventual conclusion, I intended to have already made a big course change in how ten thousand men thought about women and treated them in my workplace.

I did not consider Lieutenant Commander Peters and his secretary an issue that needed legal expertise to resolve. They were a leadership problem. Leaders exist to make these differentiations. By the time I left San Diego I had built the first childcare center in the Navy (from coke machine receipts after the Navy rejected a building request) and set a completely different tone for women in the Navy on the West Coast. We had industry leaders and politicians from all over the West visiting to see why our women were so positive and performing at such high levels.

Second case.

In the 1980s, those of us responsible for all the American sailors in the half of the globe that encompasses Africa, Asia, and points in between were starting to see isolated cases of a new sickness. It was being called AIDS. We were worrying about a lot of other military threats at the time, such as the Russians, the Chinese, and the situation in Korea. But the Russians were also eating our propaganda lunch, accusing the United States of germ warfare, specifically with spreading AIDS, so this strange sickness was high on our interest chart.

The Seventh Fleet couldn't get any support on the subject back at the Pentagon. The disease fell into a valley of political disinterest. It appeared the sickness primarily affected gay men. There were not a large number of politicians or senior military officers at the time who supported gays in general and gays in the military in particular. From the little we did know, AIDS was mysteriously targeting gays so nearly everyone assumed it must be transmitted through some sort of sex act.

As a matter of routine, in the Seventh Fleet we periodically sent teams to inspect the ports and cities in which we intended to moor ships for liberty or presence visits. About the time we were becoming concerned about AIDS, one of the teams returned with the report that everyone in Kenya appeared to be dying of AIDS! That may have been an exaggeration, but we cancelled all port visits to that part of the world until we could make a further determination. We dispatched another team, this one led by our fleet surgeon, Dr. Bill McDaniels, an exceptional leader himself, who would later be promoted to admiral. Bill visited Kenya's port city of Mombasa to personally review the situation. Soon he returned with the confirmation that the entire country of Kenya was essentially dying of this "wasting" disease.

From his observations and medical contacts in the Far East, Bill was convinced that AIDS was about to be a major problem throughout the Seventh Fleet operating area. He and I discussed what we knew or suspected. We assumed AIDS was passed by a sex act. We knew that a number of our sailors frequented prostitutes. We suspected that a certain percentage of our sailors were gay. We knew that some young sailors got so drunk they sometimes had no idea of the sex of the person they were having sexual relations with.

Did we like the logical results or morality of this? Doesn't matter. Those were the facts and we didn't want to reinforce the Russian disinformation campaign. Nor did we want Americans to inadvertently be the source of infecting our allies' citizens. There was a possible line of attack, for Dr. Bill had located an expensive blood test for the AIDS virus. This is one of those cases where expert advice is absolutely essential to good leadership, and Bill provided the medical recommendation that we test every sailor in the Seventh Fleet and relocate those that were ill back to the United States. That way they wouldn't be infecting allies and they could get the care that they would eventually require. Our boss, Vice Adm. Paul McCarthy, agreed with this approach.

Before we could begin, we received contrary direction from the Department of Defense: "AIDS is not fatal nor a major medical problem; it is not necessary nor appropriate to test all sailors." To make sure we didn't misunderstand this direction, the four-star admiral in charge of the Pacific Fleet directly called Bill at home to berate him for not following the party line. If this is not reminiscent to the flakey guidance the country received during the Covid-19 pandemic, you have not been paying attention.

It is possible that in the long history of the Navy, this directive and personal message to the fleet surgeon ranks at the very tippy-top of wrong-headed and stupid official positions. It was a consequence of the AIDS virus stumbling across the cultural tripwires of gays in society and in the military. Out on the tip of America's spear, however, in our daily face-to-face engagement with the Soviet Union, we couldn't be constrained by such nonsense. From the flagship's stateroom, our boss, Adm. Paul McCarthy, called the four-star admiral. He was Paul's immediate boss: "Admiral, we firmly believe the Department of Defense guidance is an error, and the message we have issued to the Seventh Fleet will stand."

Bill and I couldn't hear the other end of the conversation, but we both took a half-step back as the tirade boiled harshly off the telephone. Then our boss said, "Sir, if you wish, you can relieve me and put someone else here who may do what you ask."

There was another mishmash of noise from the phone before it went dead. Admiral McCarthy hung up and looked at Bill. "Doc, I sure hope you are right!"

We instituted testing, and whenever we obtained a positive result (the largest number were from the crew on board our flagship) we shipped the sailor back to the United States. In the States, the individual would get the best medical care. There he would also not be a potential American ambassador of disease.

Time proved our fears and actions to be well founded.

What does this case study delineate? Leadership remains a contact sport. All decisions require the assumption of risk. Individuals with

Vice Adm. Paul F. McCarthy Jr. took politically unpopular stands when the correct course best served America. *U.S. Naval Institute photo archive*

specific occupational skills (doctors, lawyers, etc.) often assist a leader and significantly reduce decisional risk. Other times functional advice can be distracting rather than helpful. There are no simple answers when you are dealing with transformational events.

PART 4

Special Approaches for Senior Leaders

29 ★ BROKEN LIGHTS

AMERICA MAINTAINS MANY MILITARY and diplomatic outposts throughout the world. This is appropriate. We would much rather face our enemies in foreign lands than on the rocks of Connecticut or the beaches of Southern California. Each U.S. outpost, however, inherently carries a potential downside. Physical presence brings the very real danger of being sucked into taking sides in local politics—in matters of critical importance to the host country that have little or no impact on U.S. interests—where involvement would weaken the United States. Vietnam and Iraq are only two historical examples where our representatives sometimes failed to draw this key distinction.

Frequently the people who seek to involve us are both intelligent and motivated. There is good reason. Their survival is at stake. They appreciate the local balance of power and understand its politics better than we ever could. They often have carefully studied the one great power in the world. And we have a well-known weakness: Americans pay extraordinary weight to catchphrases. We are often easily fooled by emotional words like communism, liberal, Muslim terrorist, socialism, and fake news.

This case study deals with events in the Philippines in 1985 and 1986. To historically place the reader, the Vietnam War had ended ten years earlier. The Cold War was going to last another five years.

In 1985 Ferdinand Marcos had been president of the Philippines for twenty years, the last thirteen under martial law. President Marcos had risen to political prominence as a result of his personal record during World War II of fighting with the Filipino rebels against the Japanese. His firm actions against communists and Muslim extremists, along with his support of the U.S. military bases in the Philippines, had earned him strong and unwavering backing from the U.S. government. During the 1980s, however, there had been a growing series of accusations against Marcos and his wife that referenced spending excesses and revolved around about the worsening Philippine economy.

As in real estate, "location, location, location" is important in understanding a nation-state. The Philippines occupy a unique position in the critical South China Sea area. The country was used as the primary Navy and Air Force staging point for Vietnam. The great port of Subic Bay and its Cubi Point Naval Air Station were the forward repair site for the Seventh Fleet assets engaged in Vietnam. The nearby Clark Air Force Base had provided most of the logistics support for the Air Force assets engaged in Southeast Asia.

By the mid-1980s Subic Bay was no longer the principal maintenance site for Seventh Fleet ships. That load was now shared with the facilities in Guam, Yokosuka, Sasebo, Chinhae, and even Hong Kong. But a great deal of ship repair was still done at the Cavite Shipyard in Subic, and Clark remained the largest U.S. overseas military base in the world. Consequently, the Seventh Fleet flagship, the USS *Blue Ridge* (LCC 19), visited Olongapo in Subic Bay frequently. In 1983 and 1984 I had been in charge of the submarines in the far Pacific. I was now the chief of staff of the Seventh Fleet. During the three years we had lived in the Far East my spouse would fly into Manila every few months for formal social events. On one such weekend, as we were on our way to the Philippine Palace to represent the Seventh Fleet admiral, she noted, "There are fewer lights and more potholes every time we come here."

I reflected for a moment. Her fresh eyes were correct. Even in the best parts of town the working streetlights had become so few that they were nearly obscured by the large numbers of large-winged moths that circled each glowing bulb.

Later that same evening, President Marcos gave me a new demand. He informed me he wanted fifty new U.S. Army trucks for the Philippine army. He said he needed them immediately if he were going to continue to keep the Philippines safe from communism and Muslim terrorism! He maintained he had the full support of the American ambassador. To support that, he called our ambassador over to where we were standing by one of the four bars. The latter acknowledged that he had already sent a dispatch back to the State Department supporting the foreign military sales truck request. I told them both I would staff the issue for my admiral, Vice Adm. Paul McCarthy.

I already had my own opinion on the subject. The Seventh Fleet staff routinely sailed on board the USS *Blue Ridge* to nearly every Southeast Asian country. There was a normal pattern to our four- or five-day visits. The first evening we held a reception for two hundred to four hundred of the host country VIPs. The second and third evenings the senior officers were entertained in smaller gatherings. The fourth evening many of us went into the bush (sometimes literally) and had beer with the opposition. The next day we would get under way for a new port, comparing notes and developing new intelligence assessments in the process.

Thus each of the twenty senior officers on the Seventh Fleet staff had lots of time walking in the Philippine rain. I had already polled the senior staff. None of us believed there was a communist or Muslim threat in the islands. The Cold War was ongoing, but communism appeared dead, dead, dead in the Philippines. If the ambassador and his CIA officer didn't understand that, that was due to their own inadequacies, but they reported to the State Department. Our reporting chain ran up through the secretary of defense. The dual reporting chain to the president was a clear advantage for the president, for he was not dependent on the weakness of one ambassador or inadequate CIA station chief (as I certainly believed was the case in the Philippines).

We thought there was lots of mismanagement, malfeasance, bribery, and theft in the Philippines, particularly in the Presidential Palace, and certainly some friction between the major islands (e.g., the people in Cebu hated anyone from Luzon), but the latter situation had existed for decades. We knew some Filipinos were being killed in the jungle, but we had no idea who exactly was pulling the triggers. I was personally suspicious as to why Marcos suddenly wanted trucks. We didn't want the United States to become enmeshed in a problem with only local origins, and we weren't interested in handing out weapons that soon might be turned against U.S. soldiers.

The problem is that low-level-technology countries are actually difficult to peer into and spy upon. You normally need human assets rather than technology. Was there really a communist threat? We brought in two spy ships to circle the main island of Luzon and suck up the communications spectrum. After a month we had nothing, no manifestos, which was good, but nothing else, which was bad, because it implied that any anti-Marcos orders were being passed face-to-face and by cell phone. In the meantime, the Filipino deaths continued in the forests. And Marcos was still pinging on the ambassador, raising the chant that the threat was the communists.

A Filipino who had gone to West Point with one of our Army officers was drinking beer with him at the Tomahawk Club in Olongapo. Our guy thought his friend got a funny look on his face when he mentioned something about "the Filipino army retirement system." Right about then the Shore Patrol made its nightly raid on the club. Afterward, the Filipino officer no longer wanted to talk about the subject.

I finally dispatched a small polygroup of Marines, special forces, and my best interpreters to wander into the forest near where several people had reportedly been killed. Their tasking was to see what the hell was going on.

It turned out the forest villagers were very interested in a neutral ear! They reported they had been been under siege for years! The basic problem, contrary to what we had been told by the palace, was that there was no Philippine army retirement program for any rank or rate junior to a general. When generals retired, they got a generous sum plus the allotment of a specific portion of the national forest as their domain. The army officers and men got nothing but the relationships they had developed. If those had been good, after they retired the officers would journey to the civilian headquarters of the general they had worked for in uniform. There they would be put to work logging, cutting, shaping, and shipping mahogany and other rare woods, as well as protecting the other ex-soldiers from the villagers whose livelihood they were now poaching.

According to the word in the forest, the new trucks President Marcos was requesting were intended to make it easier for the retired soldiers to drive competitors from their illegal logging sites in the national forests. The reported "communists" that were being killed were not ideologues, but rather other hungry Filipinos.

Nevertheless, when we shared our information with the American embassy, the American ambassador was not convinced. President Marcos continued to push him for trucks, a request the Defense Department stalled. On the domestic front, Marcos called for a "snap election" to solidify his political base. During the previous election, Marcos had assassinated his primary competitor. This time, the spouse of the assassinated man was Marcos's main opponent. She was brave to oppose him, but from our perspective she was not an ideal candidate as she wasn't overly fond of Americans.

As election emotions heated up, a real problem developed for the Seventh Fleet. The United States had been in the Philippines for a long time. The climate is gentle and living is inexpensive. There were a quarter-million American citizens, mainly retired military (former Seventh Fleet sailors), living amid the fifty-four million Filipinos. The Americans were intermingled with the Filipino society—living cheek to jowl—but were very visible, as most of the Americans were several inches taller and many pigment shades lighter or darker than the native population.

If general violence broke out and turned nationalistic, we did not have sufficient assets to protect our citizens. And domestic violence was definitely increasing. We made plans to evacuate as many as possible to one of the islands in Manila Bay. But we needed as much advance notice as possible if events were going to turn south.

We held our breath (and moved all available Marines and their helicopters to the Philippines) through the pre-election campaigning. After the election was over and Marcos had won, instead of proceeding with governing, President Marcos became even more erratic. Among other things, the truck issue was apparently driving him nuts.

We decided we needed better information on what he was planning. NSA satellites weren't going to provide it, because no one in the Philippines was using sophisticated communications devices. Spies didn't seem to help. We decided to tap the palace phone system.

The U.S. terminus was in an unused room on the same deck of the USS *Blue Ridge* flagship as my office. The entry into the room with the recorders was from an adjacent room so that no one in the ship's passageway could see anything unusual. Inside the second room, four eighteen-inch reel-to-reel machines began slowly revolving every time one of the key palace phones was picked up. Two uniformed men in headsets sat on red Naugahyde benches in front of the machines and sampled the conversations. After the first few days, the senior intelligence officer had decided he was not interested in being alerted to simple discussions of bribery, political chicanery, and mistresses. We could waste all day listening to these aspects of Filipino internal affairs. We were only concerned about the welfare of American citizens.

Then one evening, we suddenly had something that made all the risks of installing the taps worthwhile. Although the announced vote had not been that close, there had been accusations of election irregularities. These claims were being supported by some of the religious leaders in this solidly Catholic country. In the middle of the night President Marcos made a fateful decision. He personally picked up his palace telephone and ordered the assassination of his defense secretary (Juan Ponce Enrile), the chief of staff of his army (Fidel Ramos), and the woman (Cory Aquino) he had just defeated at the ballot box!

Fortunately we were listening.

One of the Seventh Fleet staff officers had attended West Point with General Ramos. He had the general's personal cell phone number. Arrangements were hurriedly made. Before assassination teams could arrive at the three residences, Navy helicopters had beaten them there. The man who had been Marcos's defense secretary for more than a decade went back to his home province. He believed he had much more support there than did Marcos. General Ramos insisted on "going to ground" by taking control of loyal components of his army. We put the rest of the family members and Ms. Aquino on a Navy ship and sent it to sea far away from any cameras or reporters.

Ms. Aquino's supporters began massing in the countryside. Soon there were crowds of several hundreds of thousands waiting on a leader. Enrile and Ramos announced their support for Ms. Aquino. The crowds grew even larger. Three days later, Ms. Aquino was surreptitiously landed and the bloodless revolution in the Philippines was on.

As a man who had been president for decades, Marcos had a good feel for populist politics. He knew the tide had turned against him in the Philippines and he fled.

If you can ignore emotional labels—like "that's communism" or "fake news"—intended to shortcut thinking, and are able to absorb the emotional strain that accompanies risk taking, you may actually do some good now and then.

30 ★ SPEAKING TRUTH TO POWER

LEADERSHIP CAN BE SIMPLE. You devote time to learning a discipline and finally appreciate that timely decision making is as important as situational appraisal. There is not much more to it. It may be why the military produces so many good leaders. They provide time for their future leaders to "season." The military services don't try to bring people straight in to the top.

That's not always true elsewhere. Many seem to believe a good leader can prevail anywhere. Perhaps, if he or she is really exceptional and a good listener, but so few are. And the problem is that not all facts needed are readily observable. Leaders need information, lots of it. Poor "leaders" often have personalities that erect walls against the flow of critical advice. The secretary of defense during the 2003 Iraqi War, Don Rumsfeld, frequently personally conducted briefings on the Iraq War. His unique and forthright style either charmed or fascinated the press. It makes him a great leadership example. I worked directly for him before and then again during the war. There are few people I have ever met who are as intelligent, charming, vivacious, talented, and energetic as Don Rumsfeld. I thought he was a superman!

At the same time, I could see his results and they often were not terribly good. I many times wondered why he was not more effective.

Don Rumsfeld should have been immensely popular in the Defense Department. The secretary had all the tickets. He had served in the Navy. He had previously been the secretary of defense. He was a Republican in the Bush administration that followed the unpopular (in the military) Clinton administration. Senior military officers are relatively conservative, as was Rumsfeld personally, and Rumsfeld significantly increased military funding as well as retirement pay for senior generals and flag officers. Didn't the Republicans cement a senior military loyalty that was theirs to begin with? Isn't the military sworn to respect civilian leadership, no matter what the party brand? Don't they?

Well, yes, they are and do, but the secretary's particular leadership flaw cut through that trait. He tended to make enemies of the senior officers, and he made more foes than he could afford.

To understand this, let me go back to the day Secretary Rumsfeld held his first staff meeting in the Pentagon. There was only skeleton staffing in the Pentagon. I was the lone political appointee holdover from the Clinton administration, probably because I was a retired admiral and thus seen to be less "political." I also was not in an obvious "policy" billet. Instead I was running the technical organization of several hundred thousand people who procured the weapons and services needed to keep the military operating. Secretary Rumsfeld called in the four of us who were at that time his only direct reports, along with four or five of his personal staff.

As soon as you met him, you instantly knew how he had managed to be a congressman, White House chief of staff, and a two-time secretary of defense, and how he had made millions in industry. Secretary Rumsfeld had a commanding presence and was well prepared. He had several action items for each of us. I jotted mine down on the notebook I had brought with me.

When he dismissed the team, I maneuvered to be the last person out of his office. Experience had taught me that there was a much greater chance for my next step to be successful if there were no witnesses. As the person in front of me exited, I closed the door on the individual's heels and firmly held it closed, turning around to face the secretary, who had seen us out. There was now no one else in the oversized room. "Mr. Secretary, item three on your list to me doesn't make sense. I don't want anyone to know you even considered it. It will make the new administration look foolish. I don't intend to have anyone else know about it and I'm going to forget you asked. I will work on items one and two and get back to you on those within forty-eight hours."

Rumsfeld was about a foot away from my face. He had been a championship wrestler and was still in great shape. He stared in my eyes and seemed to lean forward on his toes.

I kept eye contact with him. He swayed wordlessly back. I opened the door, turned, and stepped out of his office.

The secretary never again brought up item three. In the rush to get the Pentagon organized, no one else on his staff appeared to remember the item I had deliberately dropped. In a later conversation, Don

Rumsfeld said to me, "I cannot tolerate someone standing up to me, but if they don't, I won't respect them." After that first day, the two of us worked well together.

But what about the men and women in uniform who actually make the Defense Department work, the chairman of the Joint Staff and the chiefs of the different services? How did these individuals interact with Secretary Rumsfeld?

There are more than a handful of gadflies in the public arena that are attracted to defense issues, and goodness knows there are always a number of controversial military matters. At the same time, each new administration often wants to place its mark on the portion of the budget that spends most of the discretionary dollars, which is certainly their right. Secretary Rumsfeld was particularly interested in ensuring that the Defense Department was transformed to be better ready for the threat he saw in the new world. He believed the United States needed a more mobile and flexible force.

He was clear that he had adopted this as the mission for his term. He also believed that he could do a better job than the current military leadership in personally selecting the future senior admirals and generals. To accomplish the latter, he had recalled his military aide from his first tour as secretary to assist him in the process. The latter was probably a bridge too far.

Several of the current chiefs believed that the secretary was more receptive to the gadflies and a retired, out-of-date admiral than he was to the chiefs of service who had more current relevant military experience and who actually knew the flag officers and generals in their services.

I believe Secretary Rumsfeld's personal need to always be the only top dog caused him to pick fights with each of his service chiefs and chairmen over issues on which their decades of personal military experience had given them unique perspective. Despite his early years of active duty Navy service and subsequent Reserve service, there was no way Secretary Rumsfeld could acquire their equivalent experience. That does not mean the uniformed officers' backgrounds gave them the right answer for all their judgments. And it was certainly Rumsfeld's role to look for "revolutions in warfare" (the previous administration's keywords) or "transformation," which was the term in vogue during his administration. And clearly different conclusions could be drawn from the same data. But driving real change would have required careful listening on the part of the secretary. And sometimes senior military officers are human and get tired of fighting each and every issue through a facade of indifference or active intolerance.

And then there was the foolishness of Deputy Secretary Wolfowitz. The latter briefed President Bush about going to war in a country that held no national interest for the United States, and Secretary Rumsfeld insisted (in order to demonstrate the correctness of his new "mobile" policy) that the Army would conduct that war with only a third of the troops the Army chief of staff believed necessary. I am not sure that Secretary Rumsfeld and the Army chief of staff ever sat down and talked with one another about why they believed in different numbers. Thus, neither had the opportunity to realize one was speaking about the war-fighting phase and the other was talking about the peace-keeping phase. Although the president backed his secretary, the senior military audience, all of whom were following this in the papers, was not stupid. Even though the administration was busy telling everyone the troop decision was not wrong, nearly everyone in the Pentagon, the Army, and all the other services knew that answer was wrong (before, during, and after the invasion, when postwar events proved it so). But everyone in the administration continued to beat their breasts. I was watching this from the inside. A third of my people would be injured but I could not get anyone to alter their path. No one was interested in making anything work, in keeping people from being killed in Iraq; the administration wanted to be proven right about the number of soldiers!

This decision and others like it poisoned the communications environment within the Department of Defense. During the Rumsfeld and Wolfowitz era, information flow up and down the chain was seriously impeded. This included all intelligence, including tactical information about the war in Iraq.

I will give you a specific example of the latter. Paul Wolfowitz, speaking for the president, asked me to go to Iraq. I arrived in early June 2003 and immediately became the finance minister of Iraq and director of management and budget of the Coalition Forces for Ambassador Paul Bremer. After a few months, I made a trip back from Iraq with Ambassador Bremer to ask Congress for additional funds. The morning before we briefed the Senate we met in the Pentagon to ensure that Secretary Rumsfeld (Jerry Bremer's titular boss) did not have any last-minute questions. I mentioned one of my current concerns to the secretary. "Do you realize many of your soldiers in Iraq don't have armored vests?"

The secretary concernedly turned to the chairman of the Joint Chiefs, who was standing with the two of us. "Is that true?"

The chairman nodded. "Yes, I haven't told you because it isn't important. The soldiers not on patrol share their vests with the soldiers going on patrol."

I shook my head. "That's not true. No one shares his armored vest in Iraq. Unlike some places we fight, there are no safe zones in Iraq. Everyone needs an armored vest at all times. Every soldier is subject to being fired upon at any time. My wife is out and about in Baghdad every day doing work for you. She doesn't have any protection. Neither do I. Neither do 30,000 of your soldiers, Mr. Secretary."

This had been an issue in the field for four months and the chairman had yet to inform the secretary! This specific news would break in the *Washington Post* two days later. And the secretary of defense would have been clueless without his chance conversation with me!

After a history of communication failures like these on both sides, the extended public and private disagreements between Rumsfeld and the chiefs began even to erode the centuries of the military's unquestioned acceptance of civilian control.

A year later I was sitting with a reporter having lunch when he had to break off our discussion. He told me the weekly "tank" meeting between the secretary and the heads of each of the services in the Pentagon was scheduled to end about now. The reporter explained to me that the secretary of defense had previously directed each four-star not to disclose their discussions and had them sign nondisclosure agreements. I then watched as my lunch mate received multiple phone calls from "tank" participants explaining their individual views of what had been said about the items on the secretary's agenda. The reporter told me he didn't intend to use any of their information because he didn't feel the military should be going behind the secretary's back. I later wondered if he regretted that decision when it became evident how dysfunctional military-civilian relations in the Pentagon were during those days and when critics began asking why the Pentagon press had not been doing their job to track this widening crevice.

The nation's senior uniformed military team had come to distrust the brilliant and proven manager who had been appointed by the president and approved by the Senate. Why? In my view, Don Rumsfeld's need to always be right had severely inhibited the free flow of unwelcome but necessary information within the Pentagon. That one flaw overrode all the grand talents the two-time secretary of defense brought to the game.

Having to always be right is a terrible impediment to good communication.

It is challenging for subordinates, even those who should be strong leaders themselves, to gather sufficient courage to speak truth to power. Anyone who aspires to be a leader should strive not to make the communication process more difficult.

31 ★ LESS CAPABLE PEOPLE

HOW DRIVEN DOES A leader have to be?

Not nearly as much as you think. I work hard to keep my personal tachometer well below my mental red line. It's not that I don't enjoy the chase. No, I'm the usual adrenaline-addicted, accomplishment-addled workaholic who wants to be in charge. But after I left the cushy confines of school, I soon learned it was a serious mistake to ever work close to my full capability. Instead, a leader needs to be ready and able to surge energy and shift attention in the middle of the night. If you don't have a reserve, life's daily minutiae will have depleted your stamina just when problems that demand real leadership pop up.

Working too close to your capacity carries with it several related downsides. We have all seen leaders who lack the flexibility to take disappointments in stride. They don't focus on the problem. They may lose their tempers. They don't recognize when their subordinates are sending nonverbal messages. They miss the personal indices of intense disagreement—the stuttering, tics, behavioral changes—that a less-stressed manager would intuitively notice.

Actually, it is often easy to pick out those working too near their own limits. They are the mean ones.

When I was beginning my career, the sons of bitches were the first ones I noticed. And golly there were a lot of them, more than I had expected. At the time, I was working in the early years of nuclear submarines. It was a field both technically and physically challenging. It involved real life-and-death decisions and the heavy moral weight of nuclear weapons. Not everyone, even those of us who were involved, was completely comfortable with the whole spectrum of our work. Some of our leaders were open and inclusive and drew others in to help them make decisions. Others, like a basketball player working for a defensive rebound, used nastiness as a way to box other people away. In the workplace, these big men made life sizzle! Yet they weren't unpleasant all the time or to everybody. Nearly always the individual was someone with whom I enjoyed a social relationship and often today still count as a friend. It took me a long time to realize the person was using noxious behavior to hide when he was uncertain.

You are probably wondering why mean people are not automatically thrown out of every company and post. There is a sound reason. They often perform like Tony the Tiger: GREAT! It may not be what you want to hear, but it is a fact. Since our mothers told us honey draws more flies than vinegar, we instinctively expect organizations run by nasty people to be ineffective. But, with due respect to my late mother, how often have you been somewhere where success was based on who had accumulated the biggest pile of dead flies?

Most of the cocktail party talk about the value of a proper reward system is only an example of what happens when people drink too much. Many employees work excessive hours without any positive feedback. They may work harder and better within a superior compensation system—goodness knows I certainly hope so—but to be perfectly honest, I've never seen any compelling evidence. For most people, accomplishment is its own reward. On the other hand, everyone works harder when threatened, and mean people have that aspect down pat!

I am truly sorry about this fact of life, but I long ago concluded that bad leadership doesn't automatically lead to failure. A great deal of life is up to chance. No one should be shocked if the tooth fairy sometimes shows up at the wrong pillow. Nevertheless, even if fear gets short-term results, it has distinct shortfalls. To begin with, it tends to constrain imaginative thinking. A whip doesn't serve well as a leadership guidon flagstaff. Fear has a limiting long-term effect, for no matter how loud the shouting, humans are human and successive adrenaline rushes get shorter and shorter. Finally, if a tense situation shows no signs of ever abating, people inevitably "vote with their feet," and the talent level in the organization begins an inexorable slide.

I will give you a practical example. Once upon a time the nuclear submarine force was rapidly expanding, from four bases to more than ten around the world. While the leaders had successfully established a baseline of quality benchmarks, they realized they needed a program of routine inspections that would begin a process of first maintaining and then continually ratcheting up our standards. A special group was established to make that happen. When it began, it was not much more than an idea given to some of our best people who were tasked to do what they could. No one was quite sure at the time how successful the concept would prove to be.

The group's workload was stressful and backbreaking, involving overnight travel for three hundred or more days a year. The guy selected as the first in charge of the group was brilliant, untiring, overloaded, and uncertain as to how to realize the vision. Unfortunately, the pressure of the role turned him nasty, famously so. He was mean far and wide. Even today, several decades later, if his name is mentioned, peers recall his snarl. His venom was so hot, his disapproval of any discrepancy so clear, he chased enough people from submarines that some worried the entire force might flounder for want of sufficient numbers of volunteers!

He and I locked horns. Several times. Even though he was senior to me. He knew I didn't like the way he ran his organization, did his inspections, or treated my people. I never liked him and I pushed him away from my people. But, funny thing. He was never noxious to me. Which brings up a frequent problem with mean people. Emotional bullies, like hyenas, chase organizational stragglers. And since hyenas don't go around picking on lions, members of the leadership may not even be aware of how corrosive the environment has become until the situation is in extremis. Those in the nuclear Navy let him go too far. By the time the problem was identified and the man had finally been replaced, he had imprinted his bad behavior on others. And the others were busy practicing spinning off their own little cancerous spores. Eliminating the influence and impact of mean people is not easy. Like cults, their work tends to live long after them. This problem took only a couple of years to spawn and decades to fix.

But let's talk about the more general case. What about the employee who has slipped through the hole in the recruitment and human relations process? She is already in place. No matter how limited his or her abilities, he wants to achieve. She has feelings. He needs to earn a living. She wants to deserve and receive praise. Does the mean leader realize if he keeps on yelling, the object of his scorn is going to eventually find a way to destroy himself? No? What do you think is the cause of the one-car fatal accidents, the lone motorcycle crashes, the suicides, the mental breakdowns, the serious slips and falls? What happened to cause an injury so bad the woman won't be able to return to work? Whatever else did you think would happen?

All individuals have to live within themselves. If their teammates make each hour at work unpleasant, then the majority of their working hours are spent being unhappy. One of the roles of a good leader is to adjust each individual's responsibilities until every single person in the organization can experience personal success that also positively contributes to the organization. This has been my mantra for years. It is why my teams outperform others.

The key is to always be attentive to your people and their challenges, paying real attention, not just mouthing slogans. Don't ever leave someone abandoned on an island or at a level where he or she can't cope. It may well be that there is no job within the organization that the individual can do well, or the person has already violated an inviolate organizational tripwire. If so, then get the individual out immediately without wasting time and destroying his or her psyche. Promptly deciding a relationship needs to be permanently severed is also a part of good leadership.

But there are other, often better, options an imaginative leader can use besides firing an individual when the leader discovers that the individual is in the wrong role. Each tactic is a different form of the other and is more or less useful depending on the size of the organization and the size of the leadership team. I often found one option melded seamlessly into the next:

- Assign new work. By assigning new work or projects to different executives, in a few weeks the executive roles within the teams can be subtly and significantly redefined. The stronger ones will pick up responsibilities as weaker people shed them.
- Shift responsibilities. The mentally agile executive can think of apparently logical and valid reasons to formally shift responsibilities within the organization. If you don't tell anyone your real purpose, no one will know. If you feel compelled to share all your secrets, leadership shouldn't be your business.
- Reorganize. I would like to have a winning lottery ticket for each time I have restructured an organization for one (announced) reason even though the actual purpose of rerouting was to work around a particular unyielding and stubborn bottleneck that I didn't want the (emotional or bureaucratic) expense of terminating.

In fact, once someone has become a problem and the leadership has invested the necessary time into fully understanding the particular individual's limitations, if that person has the basic talent, it is frequently the winning approach to assign the person new responsibilities that he or she can do. This is much preferable to separating him or her and consequently having to learn the capabilities and characteristics of an unknown person. Whatever you do, do not leave someone "exposed on an island" where the individual can't succeed. Give them a role or transportation off the island. Otherwise you will be ultimately responsible for what happens in their one-car accident.

And the Less Capable People for whom this chapter is titled? Those are not the individuals for whom we are developing these accommodations. No. The leaders operating too close to their own personal upper limits—the mean ones—are the real Less Capable People in any organization.

Do your damnedest to avoid joining their ranks.

There is absolutely no reason, malady, or excuse for retaining a leader who is mean. I have met more than my share of these people. None were as valuable as the good people they chased away from organizations. I don't know if the vicious people I met had been horrid all their lives. I don't know how they acted to their families. I don't know if they behaved the same way to their dogs, their cats, or their mothers. But I do know that by the time I met them their meanness had become a personal weakness.

One thing that weakness surely demonstrated: It showed the individual was overwhelmed by his or her job. It was a clear symptom of trying too hard to keep his or her head above water. These less capable supervisors had insufficient energy left for their people. Leaders often speak about people being the organizations' most important quality. Retaining mean people is a clear demonstration that the organization simply isn't serious about its principles.

32 ★ TONE AT THE TOP

EVERY GOOD ORGANIZATION HAS a shared sense of a larger purpose, a mission. If this is ever lost, cracks quickly appear at organizational stress points. This sense of shared confidence, this esprit, is difficult to recover. My experience is that as a start, it takes new leadership. It then requires at least a couple of years of special attention. In business, where outside firms are paid to look for such conditions, auditors refer to similar situations as (the loss of) tone at the top.

After I retired from the Navy, I looked for a job in the civilian sector with management and leadership challenges. I ended up going to work for a company that was at the time the largest in its manufacturing sector. As one of my first tasks I was directed to familiarize myself with the scope of this sprawling company. They gave me a credit card, a list of the sites east of the Mississippi, and a cell phone, and sent me off on my own. The first company I visited made motors for the nuclear power industry. As I walked through the plant I noticed an area where the quality margins appeared to be inadequate. I made a mental note to bring up what I had observed up with the vice president running the local operation.

My opportunity was that evening at dinner. We were at a table for eight. The other six included his deputy, his aide, and several key people from his management team. As soon as I brought the subject up, the table got very quiet and everyone looked at the big boss. The vice president picked up his glass and swirled his wine once. "Dave, you don't understand. Last year the boss at headquarters began having an affair with the wife of another of the vice presidents. Rather than her husband quitting or getting a divorce, he instead agreed to keep quiet in return for a larger annual bonus. His wife also was an employee. She was promoted. She got the only VP slot up for grabs last year. Now both her bonus money and her husband's come out of my pool. That bonus is more than half my annual pay. The tithe to my church is paid out of that money. My wife's new car comes out of that money and my kids go to school on that money. If corporate is going to screw us, we need to get our fair share some other way. So we decided this was the best way to still pay ourselves and stay within budget." At this, his direct reports at the table, who had been listening carefully, nodded, drank their own wine, cut their steaks, and in turn began to ask me what parts of the day's briefings and tours I had thought were best.

The accommodation they were making made sense to them. No matter what the big boss at headquarters and his mistress might think, there are no secrets in an organization. Of course, they were making a quality issue where none had previously existed and damaging a famous brand name that thousands of men and women had spent a hundred years building, but they were maximizing their annual bonus pool!

During the remainder of my grand tour I had a dinner on the first evening with the top management team at each place I visited. With dessert, I would again hear the same basic story about promiscuity at headquarters, sometimes with some new salacious details, which I grew to suspect were exaggerated. I would then spend the next day or two touring the facility. At some point I would realize my guide was struggling to explain that they knew a particular practice or process was wrong and that the guide personally disapproved, but it was the least destructive method of making extra money to compensate the local "tribe" for the improper dalliances that were occurring at headquarters.

I visited a dozen companies. Each subsidiary appeared to have devised its own method of cheating the central corporation. As you might suspect, the company's brand soon began suffering and the company started spiraling downward against its peers. They began selling assets. Soon the "largest in the class" was an also-ran, all basically over a high-level affair that had been "covered up."

I next went to work for Northrop Grumman and became involved in an international program to develop an immense recuperated turbine that would eventually power the Royal Navy's new aircraft carrier. In a few months I was sitting in the briefing room after the chairman of Northrop Grumman had flown into Baltimore, one of Northrop's six or seven major locations. He was being briefed on problem contracts. Northrop had just purchased an asset located in Sykesville, Maryland. The site had previously been awarded a four-year contract to construct the active sonar transducers for the Navy's newest and biggest surface ships. These transducers were each twenty-seven inches long and eight inches in diameter. They had originally been designed by Lockheed

Martin to produce powerful sound pulses in the water that would reach out literally for tens of miles searching for treacherous submarines. The tubes necessarily have to be located right at the interface of the ship's hull and the sea. One end of each tube holds an electrical connection that is in the dry part of the ship (designed to pulse the tube), and the other part of the tube couples the signal with seawater. There were 576 tubes in each shipset bundle. Sykesville had won a recompete for the contract and had previously produced twelve or thirteen shipsets of these transducers without complaint from the Navy. Sykesville was in its last year of production. The follow-on contract had already been awarded to yet another competitor.

This contract was being discussed because it was all over the news that the Navy's two newest ships, the USS *The Sullivans* (DDG 68) and the USS *Hopper* (DDG 70) were being held up in new construction due to "leaking sonar transducers." According to the *Washington Post*, when the transducers were installed they had nearly immediately shorted out from saltwater leakage. Rumor had it that a Navy commander had been tasked to start an investigation.

I was not particularly interested in the contract. It was one of the smaller ones—$18 million total with $8 million unresolved—in the Baltimore portfolio. I had my own fish to fry. The recuperated turbine was being codesigned in Sunnyvale, California, and Bristol, England. The test facility was in Bristol. I had just replaced the primary component manufacturer in California with one in Maine. It was already Tuesday and I still needed to fly to both Sunnyvale and Bristol that week. I had stopped off on the East Coast to change underwear and see if there was anything exciting in the home office. I had been dragged into the meeting because the chairman was in town and I was the only retired admiral in this branch of the company.

A comment in the room suddenly drew me away from any consideration of my own problems. The Sykesville site manager had just told the chairman that a Navy commander and a Navy chief petty officer had a conspiracy against him. He had just recommended that Northrop Grumman sue the Navy over contract violations. That would be dumb! I stood up and said, "There is no such thing as a 'conspiracy' by a Navy commander. Someone of that rank is working too hard each day trying to keep his head above water. A lawsuit by us would be like trying to kill a gnat with a hammer. It would be a mistake for our company."

The general manager of the Baltimore complex gave me a look of disapproval. He told the chairman that he and the Sykesville site manager had gone to high school together, and if the latter said something was true, one could count on it. The Northrop chairman directed his general counsel to initiate the lawsuit.

When I had left the Navy several years earlier, I had been the deputy in charge of all Navy procurement. Something was amiss. I immediately left the meeting, got in my car, and drove twenty miles west of Baltimore to the plant in Sykesville, Maryland. There I talked to the shop floor manager, walked around with him, talked to a couple of other workers, looked at the current workload, the records, the backlog, bought him a soft drink, and talked about how things were going. He was more than willing to talk to a retired admiral with a company badge. He also seemed tired of lying.

He told me the site manager's wife had been ill for a long time. The floor manager had heard she was dying from kidney cancer. The site manager was popular. He had lived in Sykesville all his life, working up the ranks at this same plant. Now he had not come in to the office for weeks. The rumor in the plant was that he was just holding on until next April when he could retire. The plant was important to the little town of Sykesville. They had recently lost several contracts they had bid on. The floor manager suspected management wasn't paying the attention they should. The plant floor was currently nearly deserted. He told me they had cut back on doing the proper quality control tests sometime after they lost the recompete for the transducer contract. One of the workers on the floor told me the government representative who checked on their contracts lived in Sykesville and liked to fish. But he still signed whatever and wherever he was told. He was there every other week instead of every other day.

The shop floor manager and I looked at the shipset of transducers that was packaged, inspected, and ready to ship to the Navy. There were already some rust spots showing through what was supposed to be a coat of impervious paint. The floor manager showed me which of the checks he suspected were being deliberately falsified.

I went back and reported my findings to the Baltimore general manager. He acknowledged what I had found but was not about to go to the chairman in California and recant or stop the lawsuit his boyhood friend in Sykesville had put into motion. The lawsuit would subsequently drag on for eight years and generate numerous unnecessary billing hours for attorneys. It would generate bushels of ill will for Northrop. The government would never discover the falsified records nor uncover any misfeasance.

I would soon leave Northrop for government to become the deputy undersecretary responsible for Department of Defense acquisition. I had an excellent vantage point from which to watch the Northrop chairman Kent Kressa (the man from California) replace the Baltimore and Sykesville management and introduce Northrop processes to restore the proper tone at the top. In fact, I would later introduce several of his methods into the Department of Defense to help maintain a proper "tone" in government.

There are a limited number of secrets and damn few conspiracies for which the truth can't be relatively easily shaken out of the nearest tree. But once an organization has wandered astray, it takes a full-bore clean-up effort.

33 ★ THE TWO-THOUSAND-GALLON PROBLEM

A LEADER NEEDS TO KNOW when to be committed.

The semidesert air of San Diego makes the city a great place to live. It has always been a wonderful place to raise a family. My wife and I and our two sons twice paused there in our traipsing around the globe. But the city also had definite drawbacks for my career. The Pacific Ocean is wide. If your mission was to keep the Russians under surveillance, starting in San Diego made for a long commute. Assuming an obligatory stop in Pearl Harbor to see the big boss, it takes nearly a month for a submarine to get on station. Each patrol was another two or three months. Then a refit in Guam or Yokosuka to fix what had broken, some liberty time (hopefully in Hong Kong or Thailand) to keep everyone interested, exercises with allies, another patrol doing our job, and a show-the-flag visit or two as needed by different foreign navies. Trying to fit everything in made it almost impossible to return to San Diego in under a year.

The United States never had enough submarines for the crews to get much time to rest and relax, for no matter what "official policy" might be, the operating Navy lives in the world of events, and during the late 1970s vis-à-vis Russia, the submarine real world was dynamic. As a consequence, the submarine turnaround times in West Coast home ports between these year long deployments were often only a few months, particularly if one or more of your sister submarines managed to run aground, bang into a buoy somewhere, or run afoul of any of the other hazards involved with operations in the deep blue sea.

My submarine had just returned from one of those long deployments. It had been operationally satisfying but we had suffered the normal wear and tear. When we pulled up alongside our San Diego repair tender we had the normal laundry list of items for which our hundred-man crew was requesting the assistance of the tender's three thousand sailors. These lists were called work packages. The lead item in our package was one I had myself placed at the very top. A nuclear submarine doesn't need much to safely operate, but the reactor and the human operators both enjoyed a sip of cool water each and every day.

Consequently, in addition to large water-storage tanks on the submarine, we had two systems on board for turning seawater into fresh water. One produced eight thousand gallons of crystal-clear pure water each day. It was a steam-powered machine of a reliable design that was installed on board every submarine in the fleet. Over the years it had proven capable of providing sufficient water for the reactor and the crew. Of course, as Defense Secretary Don Rumsfeld has noted, "shit happens," and consequently a backup machine with a quarter of its capability was also installed for emergencies. The backup machine was a completely different design (electrical), infrequently used (only when absolutely necessary), a pain in the butt to operate, and as soon as you were dependent on it, you felt in your gut that you were in extremis.

Since the backup machine produced only a quarter as much pure water as the primary unit, it provided barely enough water as the ship needed for drinking and cooking, along with the water used by the propulsion plant. In other words, no showers or laundry the minute the primary unit went off line. In addition, the *Plunger's* two-thousand-gallon evaporation suffered from so many specific problems it would try the patience of a saint. During the previous patrol it had exhausted mine! I had wasted thousands of man-hours spot-welding leaks, repacking bent shafts, and coaxing old parts to fit. When we pulled into San Diego, I had made up my mind. I would not get the ship under way again before that particular piece of equipment had undergone a complete overhaul. And I wanted to get back at sea as soon as possible to get a shot at a particularly troublesome Soviet nuclear submarine.

The leadership lesson here is simple. Once you decide what is necessary to be prepared, be prepared to do what is necessary.

Now for a little brass tack discussion as to how the Navy really operates. As much as they should be, individual submarine commanding officers are not in charge of the world. Money is always severely limited and not everyone gets what they want. In this case, I was lumped in a unit with eight other submarine commanding officers along with one tender commanding officer, a former submarine commander who had done well in command of a submarine and then had two subsequent tours in which his exceptional performance had led to him being screened and selected for "major command." The ten of us, along with a staff, reported to a squadron commander, commonly known as a commodore, who in turn reported to an admiral in Pearl Harbor.

Now when a submarine is at sea, the commanding officer has the responsibility for everyone's life and has the commensurate authority. But when you are ashore, all the commanding officers are relatively equal and the laws of supply and demand apply. At that moment there were at least four other submarines for the tender to repair. Politics are also always a consideration, and, to be candid, the commodore and I had previously experienced one or two (or maybe half a dozen) personal and professional tiffs.

After Admiral Rickover had forced the commodore to apologize to me in public some months earlier, I always thought the latter might reserve some tiny resentment deep inside. I wasn't sure my dishes quite matched his linens, so to speak. And that particular day, it would turn out that the tender commanding officer, whom I will call by the random name of Captain Stud, was also not completely aligned with me about the priority of fixing my evaporator. It turned out he was hoping to save some money on my ship to use to make some repairs to his own. So at a meeting to discuss how the tender proposed to approach everyone's integrated work package (i.e., what they were planning *not* to do), Stud told the commodore that he couldn't see keeping his people to work over the weekend to fix my evaporator. Stud elaborated that the USS *Plunger* wouldn't be going anywhere for a while and didn't need this repair as we were actually scheduled in a few months to proceed to a shipyard to begin a two-year overhaul.

These are precisely the sort of negative vibes I did not want to hear. I certainly was not interested in wasting one minute of my command time in a shipyard! I wanted to go back to sea and get another shot at that commie submarine!

If I were going to have any shot at that Russian bastard, I absolutely had to have that two-thousand-gallon problem solved! First of all, the reactor needed its daily drink. Secondly, when I made repairing the backup machine my number one repair priority, I was essentially declaring to my crew that it was so unreliable it had to be fixed before I could declare the ship was ready to get under way. There was a principle at stake. I needed all primary and backup systems in place to go to sea.

What I wanted was to be able to sail at a second's notice! My spidey sense and daily readings of the top secret intelligence reports told me there was a unique opportunity brewing! Whether I had wanted this fight over my backup generator or not was beside the point. It had found me. I sensed a unique opportunity was about to become available, and I wanted the *Plunger* to be the solution.

Because of some Russian spies (the Walker family) in the Navy, the Russians had started operating differently in the Pacific. The Russians were now routinely sending submarines to continuously patrol off our coast and thumb their noses at us. U.S. leadership was desperate to know what the Soviets were doing so we could counter them if tensions rose. The president of the United States had recently been personally briefed and was upset. And, as the expression goes, when Mama's unhappy . . .

We suspected there was a Russian missile boat in the waters somewhere off California at that very minute. It would soon be time to begin its unknown track home. Right now the boat was lost in the vast Pacific. We had the high-probability areas blanketed with airplanes. If the Soviet submarine got careless in the next few weeks and we got a sniff or two, it might give us an opportunity to call in one of our own submarines. If that happened, I wanted to be that hotshot.

My submarine had just completed a year at sea and had performed well; there could be no other crew around that was as finely tuned as a tactical team. If events broke within the next two or three weeks, we were the logical choice. But if my submarine was going to be eligible to take that mission, she also needed to be ready on the material side. To proceed on another patrol so quickly, I needed that backup evaporator. I could live with any lesser deficiencies. It was why the evaporator was number one on my list.

So I may have pushed it a bit in my comment that day at the work package conference when Captain Stud told me he didn't plan to work on my evaporator that weekend. He may have considered my comments a verbal attack when I said, "I understand why you give your sailors liberty all the time. It's so much easier than demanding they do their jobs. Since you personally have no concept of leadership, it's a simpler approach."

And Captain Stud may have said something like, "I dropped down to your engine room last night. Only pigs who can't tell a wrench from a fid wouldn't be able to make that thing make rain like Noah's flood!"

And then, since we had both wrestled at the Naval Academy and were mature officers, we may have decided there was a superior way to express our inner feelings. Which turned out to be on the commodore's carpet under the table between the legs of the other commanding officers. As I recall it (Captain Stud always remembered it differently) I had him in a full nelson when the commodore yelled down that Stud would fix my evaporator that weekend if we knocked it off!

Shortly thereafter, the Russians provided an opportunity and the *Plunger* was the only submarine ready to react. My submarine was ordered back to sea. There followed some travails and eventual success over the next year. At the end, our crew received several awards and I made a coveted trip back to Washington, DC, to brief everybody, up to and including the White House.

There was one minor complication. In the months the *Plunger* was at sea, one of the abbreviated news clips the ship received included the interesting note that my commodore had been selected for advancement to admiral and ordered to Hawaii. To fill his place, Captain Stud was being fleeted up to be my immediate boss. He was now solely responsible for my future career advancement.

I decided nothing could be gained by waiting. When we arrived in our first port, I called San Diego. "Stud, this is Dave. Listen, I wanted to congratulate you on your assignment to your new job. I can't think of anyone who could do that job better." Stud was a heavy smoker and I could hear the beginnings of emphysema in his silent breathing on the other end of the telephone. He hadn't said anything, and there was nothing to be lost, so I plunged ahead. "I think we should just let bygones be bygones, don't you?"

"Click." He hung up on me.

Eventually Stud and I would become very good friends.

Good management is for everyone. Every man or women owes it to the people he or she works with to be the best manager he or she can be. Leadership is different. A person only rarely faces the stressful environment in which leadership is necessary. Then again, an unexpected contingency may arise, and the prepared individual will suddenly find him or herself thrust forward. But remember, leadership comes with an attached price: you must actually take the steps to be prepared. In this case, I knew what I wanted the ship to accomplish and had accurately estimated that there was a good opportunity to have a once-in-a-lifetime chance to pursue a target of interest. I also had evaluated the material condition of my ship and had decided that before we went to sea for another long period, at least one material weakness had to be fixed, the two-thousand-gallon evaporator. One good management approach was to follow the approved schedule (and the path of least resistance) that would send the *Plunger* to the shipyard for her two-year overhaul. I was not interested in that route.

I could have done it differently, but not honorably. Instead of listing the evaporator first and making it the deal breaker I knew it would become with Stud, I could have pushed the evaporator down on my work package list so no one noticed. I was in charge. I could have told my staff that the lesser priority was based on my assumption that they could keep the eight-thousand-gallon unit operating (the eight thousand subsequently stayed online during our exciting chase). We were actually, however, the oldest submarine in the fleet authorized to do special operations and the one longest out of overhaul. I was not going to compromise what I believed to be the true state of the two thousand with what I wanted it to be, even if I lost my career chance against the Russian!

At the same time, I was not going to flinch. I was not going to let the fact that Stud had his own good reasons to balance his internal tender workload, and was a few years senior to me, keep me from getting what I needed for the *Plunger* to be ready. If you decide you truly need something to be prepared, move heaven and earth to get that something.

I cannot repeat enough. Leadership always comes with an attached cost. It may be unanticipated. There may be alternative paths to success. But if you decide you need to be prepared, do what is necessary to prepare.

34 ★ SOUND PRINCIPLES

THIS IS AN OCCASION ON WHICH I GAVE myself an A for effort, but a much lower grade overall. For you to fully understand the context, you will need a bit of background, and I ask you to skim through the first four paragraphs.

Have you ever driven cross country at night while trying to listen to a particular sporting contest, a country music station, or NPR? Probably not. Not with the advent of podcasts and Sirius radio. If you ever did, you would have noticed how particular stations fade in and out and you might have chased up and down the dial to recapture a particular broadcast. The physics of what was happening was that at night, the sun's rays were no longer destroying the ionosphere, that layer of charged particles that surrounds our globe fifty to a couple of hundred miles up, and AM radio waves were now banging against that ceiling. So instead of traveling straight up and dying away into black space, as they do during the day, radio programs were being reflected and reappearing, often 800 megahertz away near the other end of the radio dial.

It used to be a great way to keep yourself awake on long cross-continent excursions. Of course you needed a high tolerance for static because the atmosphere at night was also chock-full of the electronic trash that during the day the ionosphere normally let escape out into outer space. At night all these energy bursts—the lazy rotations from a passing airport's one radar beam, the cascading burst of electrons from lighting strikes in the mountains, snatches of a trucker's ribald conversation a hundred miles away, encrypted police conversations from the town we drove through several hours ago—are contained and bounce back and forth between the ionosphere and the surface of the earth. Decades ago the Federal Communications Commission (FCC) recognized this problem and directed AM stations to drop their power after dark.

Out in the oceans, down below the surface, there is no FCC to guard the sound waves. No one directs the beds of whistling and popping shrimp to be quieter when the sun goes down and the kelp beds rise, bringing all those feeding organisms closer to the top hundred feet of water. In those constrained few yards beneath the breaking surf, nothing attenuates the groaning and hissing volcanoes, the shrieking whales, or the manmade noises from the thousands of ships with unbalanced shafts and dinged screws. It is a land of constant static.

Even worse, unlike the air, where acoustic energy travels in a relatively straight line, the ocean tends to throw its weight around. Higher water density profoundly shapes the sound waves, dragging them this way and that depending on salinity (is part of the area through which they must pass near a large river?), temperature (is there a warm current curling out into a cold area?), or pressure changes (each ten feet deeper changes the pressure nearly two pounds). So while the night holds a lot of radio static, in the top hundred feet of the ocean, where the fish play, the acoustic environment is awful!

If you actually read to here, you now know more about antisubmarine warfare than most old salts!

American submariners either are or should be a little sensitive about the weapons they fire. There are lots of bad stories about torpedoes and submariners. In fact, commanding officers have a long history of being duped into carrying weapons that let them down. This started early. During the Civil War, the *H. L. Hunley* sunk twice with all hands before it finally blew itself up with its own spar torpedo. When World War II began, it was discovered that the primary antiship weapon, the Mark 14, had not been given live testing, and it had four major deficiencies. Skippers were lucky to get 10 percent kills from perfect setups! Unfortunately, the admiral who had been responsible for the weapon design and testing was in charge of the U.S. submarines operating out of Brisbane, Australia, against the Japanese. You can only begin to imagine how tortuous and difficult his assignment made the process of problem recognition and recovery.

It took three war years for the submarine force in the Pacific to determine fixes for those torpedo flaws, but when our heroes finally had a reliable antiship weapon, Japanese ships began an accelerated trip to Davy Jones' locker.

During the Cold War, the United States developed the MK-48 torpedo to replace the much slower MK-37 as our antisubmarine weapon. Nevertheless, it was a bumpy path. You may correctly assume that the MK-48 had hiccups in its development and some of those missteps may still be classified. You might also assume that since I knew how my nuclear reactor was designed and I knew how my navigation equipment was designed, I also knew exactly how the MK-48 guidance system was designed. This was not 1941, where a submarine commander accepted something that hadn't been tested and didn't work. The commanding officer of a nuclear submarine is not driving a bunch of black boxes around the ocean while barking out orders every now and then and looking surprised at what happens.

What am I leading up to? In our submarine squadron there was an annual tactical contest during which airplanes dropped submarine-like objects in the ocean. These targets were programmed to proceed at different speeds from point A to B or maybe X. And to make it more challenging, sometimes there was a squadron of destroyers working to prevent you from attacking the target, along with a few helicopters and perhaps a couple of ASW fixed-wing patrol planes. The area in which this was done was called a "range."

In order to establish a record, the underwater area of the range, as well as the surface and air above, were all instrumented. The actual position of the target, the submarine, and all the ASW assets could be known and recorded for subsequent playback later during the reconstruction.

Unfortunately, the "range" off San Diego, where my submarine and forty others were home ported, had particularly unusual acoustic conditions. Consequently, submarines undergoing their annual qualification could often detect the target, and the records of the submarine and the range all indicated they had his track nailed, but everything went to hell when the torpedo was fired. For some reason, the torpedo would not "acquire" the target. Consequently, submarines often got only three or four kills from a full load of seventeen exercise torpedoes (one always carried some warshots in the event a real-world incident, such as a Russian submarine, intruded into training).

The word about this continued lack of success gets around. Especially when it happens on boat after boat and year after year. I was not about to put up with a kill rate of 10 percent. And it turned out that we had recently been issued a new Tektronix "desktop" computer as an aid in designing sonar searches. The computer was not really terribly small—it took up more space than the largest desk on board—but for that day it was a compact marvel! And such a capability! If the computer was given the inputs of temperature and depth profiles, salinities, and different frequencies, it would generate colored images of the most probable underwater sound ray paths. Not only was this beautiful, it was information made in heaven for our immediate weapons problem. A MK-48, while it was running through the water, was nothing more that a sonar sensor looking for a sound path to ride home to its target.

My sonar officer, Lt. A. B. Johnson, took some time to think about how he could best use his new machine to determine what might be unusual about the "range." The machine generated the images slowly, giving A. B. time to mentally think about why a limit curve was bending a particular way, as well as get a fresh cup of coffee between generated displays. Then he would revise his entering parameters, push the start button, and watch while a different answer developed. And after a day or two and lots of cups of coffee, A. B. came to me and we bounced around what he had theorized about the water in our area and what we knew about the MK-48 design. By now he was postulating that the "cold California current and warm California sun" were creating much different conditions than those off Rhode Island or in the Tongue of the Ocean, where the MK-48 had been developed. We pulled out some more references. We did some more study. We spread out the design prints for the MK-48. Then it was time to either make some minor modifications to the circuitry to give the weapon a fair chance, or adjust the water. God had dibs on one.

The following week we fired seventeen exercise weapons. The *Plunger* achieved sixteen hits. Our observer was full of praise and on the spot declared us the winner of that year's tactical award.

I may have mentioned elsewhere that my boss, the commodore, and I sometimes did not view everything from the same precise perspective. We had previously clashed over several issues. I think he thought I was a "hotdog." I may have believed that rather than managing a squadron of attack submarines, he would be much more comfortable drinking tea and playing canasta for kitchen matches with my maiden Aunt Ruth.

In this case, once he discovered that we had made some minor circuitry adjustments to give the MK-48 torpedo a better opportunity against all the awful things Neptune was throwing at us in that little area off San Diego, the commodore was not completely pleased. In fact, he disqualified us and placed us last in the competition.

Later, they made Lieutenant Johnson's adjustments the standard approach for torpedo shootings on the San Diego range.

And if I had only been the slightest bit more politically astute, once the lieutenant and I had discussed what we were going to do, I would have involved the squadron deputy who was going to observe us, and then taken that individual with me to brief the commodore and invite the latter's "advice." Whatever his faults, the commodore was an intellectual, and the chances were low that he would have forbidden me from doing it. Once he was part of the problem, the outcome would have also been his. He would have publicized the outcome far and wide as his success instead of disliking me even more intensely than he already did.

So I have always given myself an A for the fact that I was not going to accept a 10 percent success rate. Think how many of my peers failed that basic test! The timing of the new Tektronix computer coming on board is just what happens more often than not to aggressive leaders. I give myself a C on the principle of acting first and apologizing later. It is a good principle, but to be completely candid, I tended to lean on the concept a little more frequently than necessary, and I may have let the commodore's imagined canasta prowess unduly influence our relationship. And my report card was all cluttered up with an F at the bottom, because it should have been so easy to have sucked him into taking ownership of our weapons shoot. He could then have had his reputation enhanced in the submarine community by understanding the physics of sound in the water of the San Diego range. And we would have still gotten our hits.

Of course, if he had forbidden us from trying or if, as he had the last time I had recommended a significant change, the son of a bitch had delayed his final approval until an hour after he knew the opportunity to demonstrate the correctness of the change had passed. . . .

Now I recall why I just went ahead. Actually, I probably should have awarded myself at least a D+.

If you must work for someone with whom you clash, force yourself to periodically seriously re-evaluate how you can interact differently. If you do not intend to vote with your feet, then you need to seriously think how you are going to change tracks. Continually banging heads wastes energy.

35 ★ A LEADER ACTS

I WAS CLIMBING UP THE SHADOWY side of a steel oil derrick, a battery-powered megaphone awkwardly slung over my back. The steel rungs were warm but not yet hot. The air temperature was already 120° Fahrenheit on its way to July's daily average of 135. My destination was a horizontal plate about a yard wide that I could stand on, still several feet above my head. Below and behind me I could hear thousands of oil workers gathering. As soon as all the shouting died down, the megaphone would be sufficient. There were no longer any loud pumps running. In fact, the lack of mechanical noise was why I was there. I paused my climb and took a look around. Vehicles were still pulling up to the temporary barricades. There was a lot of shouting but only here and there were shots being triggered off into the air. Protesters were waving AK-47s like campaign signs. That was to be expected. It was Iraq in 2003 after all. The Coalition (the United States, the United Kingdom, and Australia) had invaded on March 19 and chosen not to disarm anyone.

A week or two earlier I made my way down one of the gold-trimmed wide hallways in Saddam Hussein's former Baghdad Palace. I was making a special visit on Paul (Jerry) Bremer. Jerry was the director of Coalition forces in Iraq. Everyone in the country, including me, worked for him. I wasn't making the short walk between our offices to speak about issues having to do with my role as the senior advisor to the Iraqi minister of finance. As the Coalition was originally going to be in Iraq only for a few months, the title of senior advisor was given to the senior coalition members assigned to manage the Iraqi ministries. Instead, I wanted to convince Jerry to fire the Texas oilman President Bush had selected to get the critical Iraq oil industry back up to speed.

I intended to concede that this particular former American oil CEO might personally know a great deal about his industry, but I was going to argue that he was clearly floundering here in Iraq, where one needed portable generators to get the electricity to power laptops or cell phones and there was a paucity of gofers to constantly run to and fro to do his bidding. The reason I was making this walk was that I was receiving information from confidential sources inside the Oil Ministry that morale was awful and that the Coalition's senior advisor had lost control.

Since each of the senior advisors had been personally appointed by President Bush, replacing one was not a decision to be undertaken lightly. In addition, the oil industry was special in Iraq. It was clearly the giant of the Iraqi ministries and its smooth operation was essential to Iraq's and the Coalition's success. No matter how strong the final Senate vote had been, the U.S. Congress had only reluctantly approved the war. To demonstrate that uneasiness, and perhaps some concern for the administration's story, they had restricted our funds. While the rest of the Iraqi industries scrambled to recover, the Coalition and the people of Iraq were dependent on the Iraq oil fields to continue pumping to pay for running the critical government services. There was no backup; all Iraqi cash had been dissipated by the war. (We would uncover more pools of cash and gold later, but that is another story.) Basically, the Coalition was in the hurt locker if the oil flow was threatened for even a few days.

Unfortunately, I lost the argument that day. I won't pretend I wasn't disappointed. But that was Bremer's decision to make. Perhaps the president had tied his hands. I made my case and turned to other problems. All of Jerry's direct reports had more than a full plate!

To return to my morning on the derrick, that special meeting with Jerry had been a week earlier, ages ago in what we had begun referring to as "Baghdad Time," where often in the afternoon you could not remember the problems you had addressed in the morning. Two hours earlier Jerry had called me down to his office. He gave me a sketch of the problem on my cell phone to get me moving: the oil workers were all on strike, oil production was shut down, some fires had been reported in the fields, and armed men were demanding to meet with the Coalition leaders! When I reached Jerry's office, the Oil Ministry's senior advisor was standing with his senior staff in the office. The Oil Ministry advisor apparently had no recommendations. Certainly none of the Oil Ministry staff appeared eager or even ready to go out among a group of rioters!

Jerry needed someone to fix an extremis situation. My old man had been a labor leader. I had walked three strike lines with him (he carried me on my first) in Indiana. I had learned a bit from watching strikers break off from snowy picket lines to warm their hands at wood fires blazing in oil barrels cut in half. The first step to solving the problem was for management to understand the workplace. Unfortunately, that world was now beginning to burn, but it couldn't be as miserable as an Indiana February!

Jerry loaned me his car and driver and Ambassador Pat Kennedy gave me a megaphone. I didn't take any soldiers or bodyguards. Was I going to be fighting or fixing? I didn't need anyone else to talk. My interpreter, Ms. Nada Alsoze, had already taught me that many Iraqis spoke English as well as I.

Which is how I came to be climbing an oil derrick in the heat of an Iraqi morning.

In retrospect, when I got to the platform and turned around to speak, the rest of it was simply good management. The leadership aspect had already happened: I was the person in an unstructured situation that others (Iraqis, Americans, Brits, and Aussies of widely varying backgrounds) instinctively trusted and thus chose to inform that the U.S. oil senior advisor was not hacking it. I was comfortable expressing bad news to power (telling Jerry Bremer that his friend and the president's choice wasn't doing the job). I had been shot at before. I was comfortable going unarmed into the oil field to visually announce "I want to learn" rather than needing to be accompanied by armed guards that might have sent an entirely different message. The final leadership aspect was that I knew I was going to have to deal with uncertainty. I fully understood that flexibility was part and parcel of walking into a burning oil field. I needed to be prepared to make specific commitments, none of which I could hope to adequately clear with Jerry Bremer beforehand.

After that it was simple. I turned around and listened. The rioters wanted respect. As soon as the Coalition had arrived in Iraq, the early directors of the Coalition Authority had introduced a pay scale to eliminate graft. The workers understood this in principle and had put up with it for a couple of weeks, but the new pay scale did not recognize that the men working the oil fields were supporting the rest of the country. The workers knew their importance. They wanted appropriate changes. Now I only speak English and hadn't been involved in the previous pay scale discussions. Most of the men in the oil field did not speak perfect English, and there were several thousand of them who had started out shooting and shouting. They were filled with adrenaline. So there was some time required to ensure I sorted out what they really wanted, considered it for a couple of minutes, estimated the time it would take to import some subject matter experts from the United Kingdom, Australia, and the States, and do the necessary coordination with nineteen ministries. I knew we needed to get the oil field back in production, so I made the mental calculations and said to everyone, "If you go back to work, I will personally guarantee you a new salary scale in thirty days."

They did. We did. And other problems filed onto center stage.

Of course, many purely administrative tasks are also interesting journeys, and if you and I ever personally meet I will explain over a beer why the White House believed the best way to make the thirty-day timeline was to send my wife to Iraq to participate in the salary negotiations. Since she is bright and charming, Ambassador Bremer and the Iraqis decided she was brilliant. After she had done the negotiations and she and I were out and about in Iraq explaining the solution, she also beguiled the head of our security, the leader of the last of the Syrian Assassins. His tribe kept us safe on the road between Sulaymaniyah and Erbil as we carried the message to the Kurds.

The head of security also was an ordained Christian Methodist. He assisted Linda and me in renewing our marriage vows before his tribe and a roaring fire in the shadows of the mountains of Iraq.

There are many situations when a leader simply has to act.

36 ★ BRONZE RULES

IN THE WORLD OF LEADERSHIP, the only golden rule is to never betray your ethics or risk your integrity. Next are bronze rules. Bronze survives, even under stress. The following is a three-by-five card of bronze leadership rules.

1. A leader knows a critical moment when he or she sees it, and a leader acts. When life gets particularly vexing, before you quit, check with your shadow. The individual most frequently needing leadership is you. Discussed in **My Shadow**.
2. A leader may have to make his or her own personal decision on a situation that may go either way. A good leader then has a plan for damage control, often a closely held plan. Discussed in **Yom Kippur**.
3. Young superstars are too often recruited with alacrity and discarded with apathy. Good bosses reflect the performances they want to see and keep their own image polished. Discussed in **Mirrors**.
4. Initial on-scene reports are often wrong, skewed by personal shortcomings and warped by adrenaline. A leader must rely on the instincts that gained that leader his or her position. If a report doesn't resonate as pure as a struck tuning fork, ask again. Discussed in **Ask Twice**.
5. Leadership involves preparing long, long before any need is evident. Preparation is the way a dangerous challenge metamorphoses into a satisfying memory. Discussed in **Preparing to Be Responsible**.
6. It is terribly difficult for a leader to look down even one supervisory level and accurately make personnel judgments. Flawed people are difficult to detect. Truly rotten people have been hiding their tracks for a lo-o-o-ong time. It is important to be continually alert for a false note. Discussed in **Looking Down**.
7. Managers prepare for routine events. Leaders make things happen. Discussed in **Hard Bodies or Leaders?**

8. If you are busy making up excuses for every time you fall short, you may miss the opportunity to improve. Discussed in **War Games**.

9. Late nights are conducive to good days. Discussed in **Early Mornings and Late Nights**.

10. Leaders prepare themselves. And they prepare themselves for the expected challenge. Is your ultimate goal a particular distance race? Or will it involve resolve? If you routinely spend an hour a day working on your body's core strength, how many minutes should you spend preparing your mind for leadership challenges? Discussed in **Daydreaming**.

11. A leader needs a system to periodically refocus herself or himself or the leader's goals. Formal systems will work. Personalized arrangements can be even more effective. What is going to remind you of your core beliefs? Discussed in **Refocusing**.

12. Humans resist change. Tenaciously. They may not necessarily have a good reason. They may not have any rationale. But the fear of uncertainty often keeps humans stuck in their ancestors' emotional ruts. Stress can lever them out and up. Stress stretches the seams of established relationships and wrinkles the social fabric. Stress pries up social barriers and provides an opportunity for a bit of good to wiggle past. Discussed in **Cold Bay Women**.

13. It is astounding how few managers have feelings for those for whom they have so much responsibility. Leaders without empathy are grit in the team's gears. Cast them out like uprooted dying weeds to shrivel in the sun. Discussed in **Bullies Are Not Leaders**.

14. Never ever let foolishness stand, no matter how high it originates. If something is wrong, it is wrong. Don't condemn yourself to live the rest of your life with regrets. Discussed in **A Conspiracy of Silence**.

15. A leader must be attentive to unusual events. A leader cannot follow the Tinker Bell policy of accepting Peter Pan's "Neverland," where leaders *never* accept the situation for as awful as it is, *never* sufficiently investigate, and *never* take adequate action to root out all the rot. It doesn't matter what supervisory rules, regulations, or tripwires exist if the leaders are not paying attention. Discussed in **Red Flags and Warnings**.

16. The sobriquet "tough but fair" often attracts young men and women who aspire to be leaders. It has a rhythm, is easily

understood, and holds out the promise of avoiding messy emotional involvement. Of course, the phrase is also an utterly inadequate method of managing and is the refuge of those unqualified
to lead. Those who manage by being tough but fair ignore the
fact that nearly everyone is trying to do their best. A leader's
primary function is to assign people to jobs they can do or tasks
they can successfully grow into. You also must do the hard work
of reassigning those who are in the wrong roles. If you aren't
doing all three, you are only pretending to be a leader. Discussed
in **Tough but Unfair**.

17. Sometime a leader has to take a risk well before he or she has
all the data he or she would prefer. In this case study the "problem" sailor turned out to be simply a confused eighteen-year-old.
The real "dirtbags" were the managers who had failed to properly
evaluate a potentially dangerous evolution. To compound management's faults, when the situation went south, the "dirtbags"
slapped together an investigation to hide the problem and consequently endangered others. Discussed in **Dirtbags**.

18. A ship's commanding officer is responsible for his or her command. Period. This singular responsibility drives the person in
charge to do what is necessary to ensure success. Discussed in
Who Is Responsible?

19. A disaster doesn't occur because of only one or two errors. That
may be what the those involved say. It well may be what immediate supervisors think. But it's absolutely wrong. An incident only
starts after four or five consecutive mistakes have been made. Not
one. Not two errors, but rather four, five, or even more. By the
time an individual is found to be behaving inappropriately, or a
ship runs aground, or any event causes unnecessary deaths or
destruction, it is well past time for decisive action. When a problem occurs, don't paper it over. Investigate until you understand
the root cause and fix it! Discussed in **Stop the Bleeding**.

20. People frequently are directed, or painfully claw themselves, into
assignments for which they are fundamentally ill-suited. Once
positioned, no matter how obvious the misfit, few supervisors are
eager to involve themselves in the emotionally messy business of
rectifying the error. Nevertheless it must be done. The memories

of your people's mistakes never retire or fade. Discussed in **Leadership and Square Pegs**.

21. Integrity remains the golden rule of any relationship or organization. Observing any lower standard has a terrible cost. Discussed in **Integrity**.

22. The military needs young people and those people are pulled from the rest of America's workforce. That means the military must lead the country in cultural change. This inevitably creates tensions, for, while younger, the military population often retains America's regional and local chauvinisms. For the military leader, these bumps and lumps are leadership opportunities. Discussed in **Leadership Approaches**.

23. Institutions need reviews by outside organizations. If this doesn't happen, particularly in those "special" groups without natural competitors, it is easy to become complacent. Which is only a short step down the serene slippery slope to inadequate. That does not mean outside reviews are appreciated. They are accepted as cordially as the devil welcomes holy water. I never went through one that did not generate some useful idea. Discussed in **Wellingtons**.

24. A team performs best when you recognize the individuality of the members. Each person perceives information and solves problems differently. The question is always: How may I best take advantage of these varied skills in my organization? There is no need for completely standard roles or responsibilities. Few notice if one or more of the common boundary lines has bulged out or been sucked in a bit. Discussed in **Line Management**.

25. The best processes in all of American industry, embedded in a technological giant too big to fail, after only a few years without exceptional leadership became a shamble of a company only good enough to serve as a fire sale to America's economic competition! Discussed in **Process Is Insufficient**.

26. One of a leader's most important tasks is to plan how change will be achieved. You may often not be able to reach consensus. Sometimes you can build understanding and knowledge to the point that people will accept a course of action as reasonable. Building a rough conviction is often sufficient. See **Alignment**.

27. Pride often makes leadership more difficult. Discussed in **What Are You Willing to Pay?**

28. Leadership remains a contact sport. All decisions require the assumption of risk. Individuals with specific occupational skills (doctors, lawyers, etc.) may often assist a leader and significantly reduce decisional risk. Other times functional advice may only be distracting. There are no simple rules when you are dealing with transformational events. Discussed in **Risk Required**.

29. If you can ignore labels—communism, terrorism, fake news—primarily intended to shortcut critical analysis and are able to absorb the emotional strain that accompanies risk taking, you may actually do some good now and then. Discussed in **Broken Lights**.

30. It is difficult for subordinates, even those who should be strong leaders themselves, to gather sufficient courage to speak truth to power. Anyone who aspires to be a leader should try hard not to make it more so for their juniors. Discussed in **Speaking Truth to Power**.

31. There is absolutely no reason or excuse for a leader who is mean. Leaders often speak about people being the organizations' most important quality. Retaining mean people is a clear demonstration that the organization simply isn't serious about its principles. Discussed in **Less Capable People**.

32. There are a limited number of secrets and damn few conspiracies for which the truth can't be relatively easily shaken out of the nearest tree. But, as the parent company discovered in this case, once a problem is established, it takes a concerted effort to repair an organization that has wandered astray. Discussed in **Tone at the Top**.

33. Leadership is not for everyone. Leadership always comes with an attached cost. It may be unanticipated. There may be alternative paths to success. But if you decide you need to be prepared, do what is necessary to prepare. Discussed in **The Two-Thousand-Gallon Problem**.

34. If you must work for someone with whom you clash, force yourself to periodically seriously re-evaluate how you can interact differently. If you can't or don't intend to vote with your feet, then you are going to have to seriously think. Continually banging heads wastes energy. Discussed in **Sound Principles**.

35. There are situations when a leader simply has to act. Discussed in **A Leader Acts**.

★ AFTERWORD ★

ASPIRING TO A LEADERSHIP POSITION is a tacit acceptance of the inherent risks. I am all in favor of anyone who desires to be a leader, but I want to leave you with some general cautions. Another short vignette may help. When I was in charge of sixty to seventy commanders who were at that time driving nuclear attack submarines, I developed a rule of 10–80–10. If we went to war, I estimated that 10 percent of my commanding officers (five specific men, each of whom not surprisingly would later become a four-star admiral) would get 80 percent of the submarine kills, 80 percent of my force would sink the remaining 20 percent of the Russian submarines, and the rest of my force would do well to get safely out of their home ports. War games and later experience confirmed my estimates. As a caution, though, all you aspiring leaders should know that I didn't expect the top 10 percent to get any recognition. If the flag went up, I never expected to see any of the five again. I knew each of the superstars would keep driving himself and his ship, making ever-more difficult kills, until small probabilities mounted up into the cruel inevitabilities.

Each super warrior would eventually be carried unheralded from the battlefield on his shield. That is the fate of warriors in wartime in command of a fighting ship. Since leadership inherently involves risk, the inevitability of loss is both the exhilaration and the consequence of a leader who joins every skirmish. But it is not imperative in peacetime. It is neither necessary nor good judgment to indiscriminately accept every dropped handkerchief. Choose your engagements carefully. Neither your position as a leader nor your character require you to strap on your armor and leap to your horse for each and every challenge. Strive to limit your battles to those for a principle, a person, or your country.

While waiting for that opportunity, do your best to grow. Too many people want to be comfortable rather than challenged. They want to live on flat spaces, with friends like themselves amid furniture upholstered to cover any sharp corners. That environment will hinder anyone's evolution! The worst case I ever witnessed was the four-star admiral whose chief of staff was his Naval Academy roommate who had been passed over for promotion many times. Yet the admiral had insisted this individual from his past be assigned as his closest advisor. The former roommate had terrible judgment. He was unable to perform the pivotal chore of dampening the admiral's own tendency to act rashly. The combination did not work well.

I deliberately never took aides with me between commands. This was to force myself to grow with each new challenge. I wanted to start each new vista with people who did not think they "knew" me. I wanted everyone at my new command to understand that my door was truly fully open to fresh thoughts. I had seen the number of valuable talents there are in the world. I therefore have always deliberately cultivated relationships with people who have different views and concepts. I grow through them.

In all of my leadership roles my only constant was that I spent a great deal of time thinking about people. This is a requirement of the position. You are using people's talents to augment your vision, to furnish know-how you don't have, and to provide the assisting hands you need. You owe them your attention. Most of your staff are neglecting themselves while serving you and the task. They are relying upon their leader to worry about them. You must do so.

All leadership rests on the two pillars of ethics and integrity. These concepts are sacrosanct. There will come a time when you will find yourself challenged beyond what seems to be human capability. The true leader will somehow find the strength to launch the saving counteroffensive. At that moment you will be buoyed by your ethics and powered by your integrity.

I wish you fair winds. . . .

★ ABOUT THE AUTHOR ★

DAVID OLIVER WAS BORN NEAR Indianapolis and attended Ben Davis High School. He graduated from the United States Naval Academy and served during the Cold War on board submarines in Charleston, Connecticut, Newport News, Pascagoula, San Diego, San Francisco, and Seattle.

After spending four years in command of his own submarine, Dave directed the operations of all U.S. and Allied submarines in the Pacific against the Soviet Union as the commander of Submarine Group Seven in Yokosuka, Japan. This was followed by duty as chief of staff of the Seventh Fleet. Following selection for the rank of admiral he became responsible for plans and policy in the Pentagon. Dave was then assigned to train all the attack submarines on the West Coast (commander, Submarine Group Five in San Diego), where he also facilitated filming *The Hunt for Red October*. He returned to the Pentagon to become responsible for planning for the Navy during the four transition years following the Cold War. In his final Navy tour, he served as the principal deputy for the civilian secretary for acquisition, research and logistics.

After retiring and working as an executive at Westinghouse and Northrop Grumman, Dave was appointed by President Clinton back to the Department of Defense as the principal undersecretary of defense for acquisition, technology and logistics. Some years later, President Bush appointed him as the director of management and budget for the Coalition forces in Iraq as well as the special advisor to the Iraqi finance minister.

When he returned from Iraq, Dave believed it was critical to U.S. interests to improve our international ties, and thus he took a job for a decade as the chief operating officer of much of Airbus's United States organization.

Recently Dave became one of the founding members of the American College of National Security Leaders, with the goal of improving the dialogue between political officials and retired admirals, generals, and ambassadors.

Dave is the author of *Making It in Washington*, as well as two other leadership books, *Lead On* and *Against the Tide: Rickover's Leadership Principles and the Rise of the Nuclear Navy*.

The **Naval Institute Press** is the book-publishing arm of the U.S. Naval Institute, a private, nonprofit, membership society for sea service professionals and others who share an interest in naval and maritime affairs. Established in 1873 at the U.S. Naval Academy in Annapolis, Maryland, where its offices remain today, the Naval Institute has members worldwide.

Members of the Naval Institute support the education programs of the society and receive the influential monthly magazine *Proceedings* or the colorful bimonthly magazine *Naval History* and discounts on fine nautical prints and on ship and aircraft photos. They also have access to the transcripts of the Institute's Oral History Program and get discounted admission to any of the Institute-sponsored seminars offered around the country.

The Naval Institute's book-publishing program, begun in 1898 with basic guides to naval practices, has broadened its scope to include books of more general interest. Now the Naval Institute Press publishes about seventy titles each year, ranging from how-to books on boating and navigation to battle histories, biographies, ship and aircraft guides, and novels. Institute members receive significant discounts on the Press' more than eight hundred books in print.

Full-time students are eligible for special half-price membership rates. Life memberships are also available.

For a free catalog describing Naval Institute Press books currently available, and for further information about joining the U.S. Naval Institute, please write to:

Member Services
U.S. Naval Institute
291 Wood Road
Annapolis, MD 21402-5034
Telephone: (800) 233-8764
Fax: (410) 571-1703
Web address: www.usni.org